experience design 1.1

Nathan Shedroff

This is an update to the 2001 book, *Experience Design 1*.
It includes updated text and numerous new examples.

ISBN: 978-0-9822339-0-0

Experience Design Books
www.experiencedesignbooks.com

Table of Contents:

While everything, technically, is an experience of some sort, there is something important and special to many experiences that make them worth discussing. In particular, **the elements that contribute to superior experiences are knowable and reproducible, which make them designable.**

These elements aren't always obvious and, surely, they aren't always foolproof. So it's important to realize that great experiences can be deliberate, and they are based upon principles that have been proven. This book explores the most important of these principles.

The design of experiences isn't any newer than the recognition of experiences. As an approach, though, Experience Design is still in its infancy. Simultaneously having no history (since it has, still, only recently been defined), and the longest history (since it is the culmination of many, ancient disciplines), Experience Design has become newly recognized and named. However, it is really the combination of many previous disciplines; but never before have these disciplines been so interrelated, nor have the possibilities for integrating them into whole solutions been so great.

Experience Design as a discipline is also so new that its very definition is in flux. Many see it only as a field for digital media, while others view it in broad-brush terms that encompass traditional, established, and other such diverse disciplines as theater, graphic design, storytelling, exhibit design, theme-park design, online design, game design, interior design, architecture, and so forth. The list is long enough that the space it describes has not been formally defined.

The most important concept to grasp is that

all experiences are important

and that we can learn from them whether they are traditional, physical, or offline experiences; or whether they are digital, online, or other technological experiences.

Experience Design

www.nathan.com/projects/experience.html

experience design 1.1

2

In fact, we know a great deal about experiences and their creation through these other established disciplines that can—and must—be used to develop new solutions. Most technological experiences—including digital and, especially, online experiences—have paled in comparison to real-world experiences and have been relatively unsuccessful as a result. What these solutions require first and foremost is an understanding by their developers of what makes a good experience; then to translate these principles, as well as possible, into the desired media without the technology dictating the form of the experience.

This book contains real-world, "offline" examples to counterbalance the online examples so that we can learn from them how to create more successful experiences in new media.

experience desig

Experience Design

Experiences are the foundation for all life events and form the core of what interactive media have to offer. One of the most important ways to define an experience is to search its boundaries. While many experiences are ongoing, sometimes even indefinitely, most have edges that define their start, middle, and end. Much like a story (a special and important type of experience), these boundaries help us differentiate meaning, pacing, and completion. Whether it is due to attention span, energy, or emotion, most people cannot continue an experience indefinitely, or they will grow tired, confused, or distracted if an experience—however consistent—doesn't conclude.

Experiences have 6 key dimensions: Breadth, Intensity, Duration, Triggers, Interaction, and Significance (this is described in detail in _Experience Design 2_). One of the most important is Duration, since we live our lives in a stream of unfolding time (see Time and Motion on pages 290-292).

At the very least, think of an experience as requiring an **attraction**, an engagement, and a conclusion. The attraction is necessary to initiate the experience. It can be cognitive, visual, auditory, or a signal to any of our senses. The attraction can be intentional on the part of the experience, not just the experience creator. For example, the attraction for filling-out your taxes is based on a need, and not a flashy introduction. However, there still needs to be cues as to where and how to begin the experience.

The engagement is the experience itself. It needs to be sufficiently
different than the surrounding environment of the experience to hold the attention of the audience or user as well as cognitively important (or relevant) enough for them to continue the experience.

The **conclusion** can come in many ways, but it must provide some sort of resolution, whether through meaning, story or context, or activity to make an otherwise enjoyable experience satisfactory. Often, an experience that is engaging has no real end. This leaves participants dissatisfied or even confused about the experience, the ideas, or

Experiences

"It is not enough to insist upon the necessity of experience, nor even of activity in experience. Everything depends on the quality of the experience which is had....

Just as no man lives or dies to himself, so no experience lives or dies to itself. Wholly independent of desire or intent, every experience lives on in further experiences. Hence, the central problem of an education based upon experience is to select the kind of present experiences that live fruitfully and creatively in subsequent experiences."—John Dewey, Experience and Education

The quality and content of a person's life is the sum total of what they've paid attention to over time.
—Henry James

the emotions they just felt. An experience creator that does not spend enough (or any) attention on the conclusion—whether through inattention to detail, boredom, or speed—has just wasted his or her effort and the audience's time.

It is possible, and appropriate, for an experience to have an **extension**, which can merely prolong the experience, revive it, or form a bridge to another experience. In this sense, a larger conclusion with greater meaning can be alluded so that experiences can be elicited. Each experience still needs a satisfactory conclusion on its own level in order to justify more time for further experiences. Lack of resolution will more likely disappoint your audience than keep their attention for more experiences. Just like serial narratives (such as episodes of television or comic books), all experiences must reward attention at their end.

Experiences are crucial to our lives and our understanding of the world, as well as to our ability to function within it. Indeed, to be creative at all requires a wealth of experience from which to draw. As turn-of-the Century educator John Dewey described in his book *Experience and Education*, there are three natural mental resources: "a store of experiences and facts from which suggestions proceed; promptness, flexibility, and fertility of suggestions; and orderliness, consecutiveness, and appropriateness of what is suggested."

Finally, it is critical to remember that **while all experiences aren't created equally, all must compete for the attention of the audience and participants.**

This means that websites don't just compete with websites, or parties with parties or environments with environments. People searching for experiences—especially if those experiences inform—will choose from various media to meet their needs. One misconception in the digital world had been that CD-ROMs and websites, in particular, somehow don't need to be as interesting, compelling, or useful as traditional experiences in the same genre—that novelty alone was enough to be successful. What most developers have found is that successful digital media are those that offer experiences unique to their medium and compete with traditional media in usefulness and satisfaction.

Experiences

One aspect of an experience that can make it surprising and amazing is that of confronting one's beliefs. When we are challenged to rethink possibilities (when our beliefs and expectations are confronted by the evidence in front of our eyes), we can have a profound reaction.

This was my experience at the Institut de Monde Arabe in Paris. On approaching the entrance, the South-facing glass wall of the building, which is also part of the entrance courtyard, appears to be backed by Arabic latticework. This isn't so surprising or puzzling, and seems like a rational interior design motif for a building representing traditions that go back over 1,000 years.

Upon entering the building, one is immediately surprised by the technological modernity of the building's interior. In fact, this building is one of the most technologically sophisticated in the world. Its mediatique is buzzing with robot arms switching video tapes into a bank of players, displaying images on a wall of monitors, each representing a different Arabic countries.

However, it is when one climbs a floor or two and approaches the South wall—this time from the inside—that one is confronted with a contradiction of reality. The latticework that easily could have been assumed from the outside is, in fact, an array of working metal apertures, some tiny, others large, in each pane of glass. The sheer number of apertures multiplied from pane to pane over the entire length and height of the building is staggering and unbelievable. Like the pyramids themselves, the amount of work involved in their creation is difficult—almost impossible—to process, or to believe.

There are nearly 20,000 working apertures that open and close automatically to regulate light into the building. The prospect of such a detailed undertaking is so difficult to calculate that I was left staring in awe, silence, and disbelief that someone, anyone, would actually attempt it. Part of my brain told me it could not exist—no one in their right mind would try; yet my eyes were informing another part of my brain. Yes, indeed, it did exist, right in front of my face.

I have rarely encountered such an experience—not just the surprise or the reversal of expectations, but the vision and determination of those who created it. When you create your next experience, consider how it might exceed not only your assumptions and expectations but those of your audience as well.

Institut de Monde Arabe

1 rue des Fossés St-Bernard (5è), Paris, France
www.imarabe.org

experience design 1.1

Institut de Monde Arabe

Seduction? In the Interface?

Seduction isn't an adjective most people would associate with a computer interface or media, but whether they realize it or not, most people have been either seduced or the target of seduction by almost all forms of media. Successful seduction, however, is a careful art that isn't easily mastered or invoked.

Seduction, in fact, has always been a part of design, whether graphic, industrial, environmental, or electronic. For many, seduction immediately connotes sex appeal or sexual enticement. The sexual connotation isn't essential, however, as the essential element is attraction and appeal.

Seduction is a portion of a field of study into the persuasive aspects of computing and other media, known as CAPTology.

I believe that it's important to view the interface as an opportunity to seduce people-- not for nefarious reasons, but in order to enhance their experience and lives.

While the Dialectizer may not be the quintessential experience, it is an unexpectedly funny one. Simply, the Dialectizer will rewrite a site on-the-fly, so the site takes on a different manner of style or personality when read. It's hard to come up with a real-world use for this application, but this website presents the ability to create a different perspective, albeit a stereotypical one, that changes the experience of every other website.

The Dialectizer

www.rinkworks.com/dialect

Seducshun? In de Interface?

Seducshun ain't an adjective most sucka's would associate wid some clunker interface o' media, but wheda' dey realize it o' not, most sucka's gots been eida' seduced o' de target uh seducshun by mos' all fo'ms uh media. WORD! Successful seducshun, however, be a careful art dat ain't easily mastered o' invoked.

Seducshun, in fact, gots always been some part uh design, wheda' graphic, industrial, environmental, o' electronic. Co' got d' beat! Fo' many, seducshun immediately connotes sex appeal o' sexual enticement. Man! De sexual connotashun ain't essential, however, as de essential element be attracshun and appeal.

Seducshun be a po'shun uh a field uh study into de puh'suasive aspects uh computin' and oda' media, knode as CAPTology. Slap mah fro!

I recon' dat it's impo'tant t'view de interface as an oppo'tunity t'seduce sucka's--not fo' nefarious reasons, but in o'da' to enhance deir 'espuh'ience and lives.

Combining choice, and a type of adaptiveness, it allows users to control their experience and spin the browsing experience into something different.

The Dialectizer

experience design 1.1

9

How many different types of experiences are there? Most likely, the diversity isn't infinite. Functionally, however, the diversity is large enough to define an incredible amount of variety. This variety forms a palette for us to both define and discover what experiences have to offer—that is, what we can learn from them as well as how we can build new variations.

One way to understand what makes experiences successful is to build taxonomies of experiences that we can identify (ultimately, an endless list). This allows us to explore what makes various experiences distinct and what makes them special. The chart on this page offers only a few of the possible attributes of experiences and matches them against just a sliver of all the possible experiences. However, they were chosen because they have presented some of the best results and have revealed some of the most important insights.

The best way to explore your own opinions and insights about experiences is to expand this chart yourself.

One of the most apparent values of a chart like this is that it makes it clear how related experiences compare in different ways. In particular, it becomes apparent that many experiences, though different in medium (such as print versus live versus digital) are similar in activity, meaning, and success. This leads to one of the most important understandings about experiences, especially digital ones—that is, all experiences compete with each other on many levels and in different media. Historically, this has been poorly understood by developers of "new media," because these developers assumed that their competition was other similar media and not all possible experiences around that topic or purpose.

For example, developers during the CD-ROM explosion rushed to create CD-ROMs on every conceivable topic—most often with dubious and misguided understandings of interactivity and of its strengths and weaknesses. What they created were mostly exotic experiences that, in the end, weren't successful for their audiences once their curiosity was satisfied. Any of the criteria on an experience taxonomy could have helped them discover what was potentially important about their products next to other experiences on similar topics in other media. For example, a CD-ROM about, say, tropical fish would clearly need to compete against other tropical fish experiences, such as television shows, scuba diving, visiting an aquarium, etc. and not merely other CR-ROMs in order to capture an audience's attention, and be successful.

The same phenomenon has occurred in the online world. So many websites that have been created that cannot compete with traditional experiences in the same milieu and fail as a result.

Experience Taxonomy

www.nathan.com/projects/experience.html

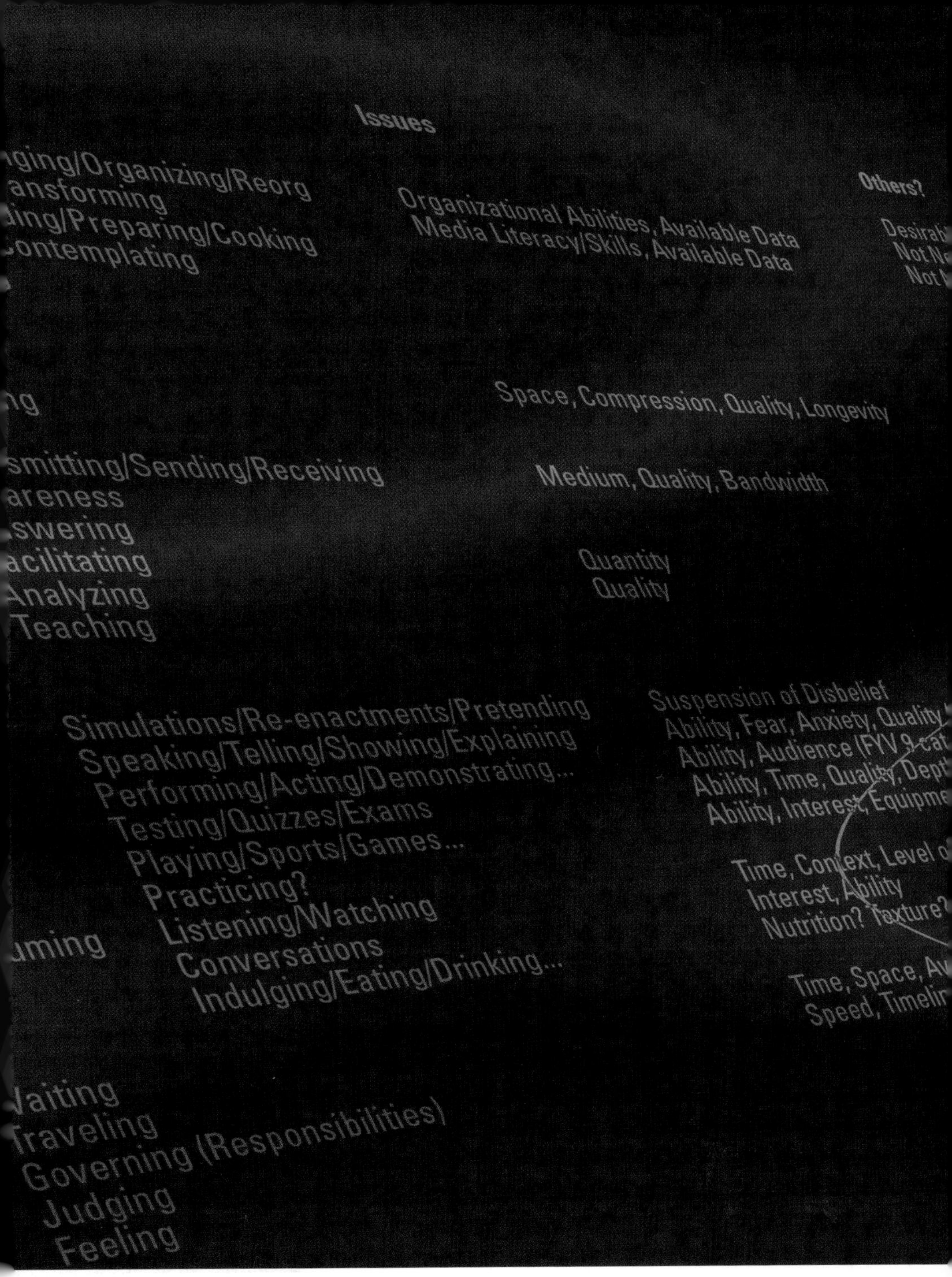

ging/Organizing/Reorg
ansforming
ing/Preparing/Cooking
ontemplating

Organizational Abilities, Available Data
Media Literacy/Skills, Available Data

Others?

Desirab
Not Ne
Not A

ng

Space, Compression, Quality, Longevity

smitting/Sending/Receiving
areness
swering
acilitating
Analyzing
Teaching

Medium, Quality, Bandwidth

Quantity
Quality

Simulations/Re-enactments/Pretending
Speaking/Telling/Showing/Explaining
Performing/Acting/Demonstrating...
Testing/Quizzes/Exams
Playing/Sports/Games...
Practicing?
Listening/Watching
Conversations
Indulging/Eating/Drinking...

Suspension of Disbelief
Ability, Fear, Anxiety, Quality
Ability, Audience (FYV 9-cat
Ability, Time, Quality, Dept
Ability, Interest, Equipme

Time, Context, Level o
Interest, Ability
Nutrition? Texture?

uming

Time, Space, Av
Speed, Timelin

aiting
Traveling
Governing (Responsibilities)
Judging
Feeling

Experience Taxonomy

Some of the happiest memories from our youth include the fun and excitement of amusement parks. Whether it was the rides themselves or just the environment, the excitement was always a result of exploring an unusual environment with often fantastical features. Most amusement rides offer us the ability to experience things we could not otherwise, or play on our senses in ways that would be difficult outside the parks. Rides that twirl us at high speed or lift us off the ground are usually novel and stimulate our adrenaline and emotions. Even walking around the park is often a visual, sonic, and olfactory treat, as we smell, see, and hear novel things created especially to grab our attention and enhance the experience.

Amusement Parks

www.nathan.com/projects/experience.html

While everything we create are experiences, events and environments (like theme parks) are, perhaps, the pinnacle of experience creation because they envelop us more thoroughly than most products and services.

Amusement Parks

Travel is a universal experience.

Whether you travel across the world, or to a part of a city you never have visited before, there's something important and magical about finding new situations and seeing new sights. While travel is often an observational experience, many travelers specifically travel to participate in the action— whether it's an extreme or action sport, or whether it is to immerse themselves in another culture directly, such as working in another country or leraning the local language.

Travel has always been experiential but an emerging segmentation of the travel market, experience travelers, is finally being defined. These are the travelers who explicitly seek-out unique experiences, across categories and price ranges, wherever they go. They are just as likely to eat at the best restaurant in a city one night, and from a street vendor the next. They seek what's unique to a place and often try to pass as a local, eschewing traditional tourist traps. They are just as likely to visit a museum for that one, rare highlighted piece that interests them, and then leave to surf, mountain bike, hike, or simply walk in a part of town not frequented by tourists. When they shop, they aren't interested in stores they can find at home, but boutiques with things they didn't know to look for. Experience travelers are a behavioral segment and, as such, cross demographic lines and categories.

This is the difference between traveling and touring. The former requires an authentic interest in new things and an openness and willingness to experience them. The latter is usually limited to "seeing" the sights—often through the lens of a photo or video camera or the window of a tour bus.. Tourists tend to gravitate to the familiar for meals and companionship while travelers abhor both, instead going out of their way to meet new people.

VirtualTourist.com is a fantastic site for both traveler and tourist, though the emphasis is on travelers, and often on adventure travel. The site excels in knowledge since it allows everyone to post their experiences, photos, stories, and travel histories for others to share. The site makes it easy to meet and communicate with others as well as to search for people who have been to the places you've visited or are planning to visit.

One of the nicest features is a visual map of each members' travels that is compiled automatically when members enter their travel histories. This map shows where someone has been, as well as where they intend to go next.

www.virtualtourist.com

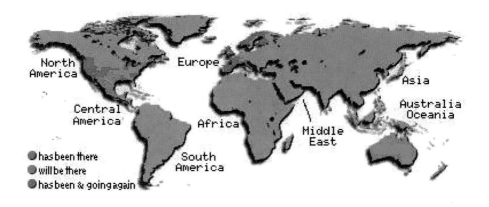

virtual Tourist
Real Travelers · Real Info

Worldwide Travel Guides, Maps, Vacations, Hotels

Search: [   ] [Destinations ▼] GO!

email to friend | help

| Home | Travel Guides | Book Travel | Meet Members | Travel Deals | Trip Planner | Forums |

VirtualTourist TRAVEL GUIDES

Choose a Destination

North America   Europe   Asia
Central America   Middle East
& Caribbean   Africa
South America   Australia & Oceania
Antarctica

Over 2.2 Million Locations

Top Spots

Paris Hotels, Things To Do	**London** Hotels, Things To Do
New York City Hotels, Things To Do	**Prague** Hotels, Things To Do
Rome Hotels, Things To Do	**Barcelona** Hotels, Things To Do
Amsterdam Hotels, Things To Do	**Bangkok** Hotels, Things To Do
Venice Hotels, Things To Do	**San Francisco** Hotels, Things To Do
Vienna Hotels, Things To Do	**Las Vegas** Hotels, Things To Do

» view all travel guides
» view special interest guides

VirtualTourist MEMBERS

260 online now
900,746 total
442 new today
search for VT members

FEATURED MEMBER

Escadora7
Lives in Los Angeles

Member since:
March 6, 2005

"Mars? Been there! Let's discover Earth!!!"

 17 countries
46 locations
205 tips

» make your own map

FEATURED DESTINATION: Barbados
Now is the perfect time to discover Barbados. Enjoy a true island getaway with endless beaches and a vibrant nightlife. Experience the authentic Caribbean. Plan your luxury vacation today.

VirtualTourist FORUM

VT Travel Forum
Ask about a trip you're planning.
VT Technical Help Forum
Help using VT, computers & more
VT Miscellaneous Forum
Fun and friendship with fellow travelers

FEATURED TRAVEL FORUM

tuamotu asks about San Francisco
Q.San Francisco: travel info

TRAVEL REVIEWS BY VT MEMBERS   1,507,138 Reviews 2,977,500 Photos

○ Read About: [Hotels ▼] In: [Paris ▼] (GO)
○ Write About:

Chiang Mai Things To Do

Wat Phra That Doi Suthep "a must!" by Wann
I think this place is a major attraction of Chiang Mai. I 've been there many times. Wat Phra That Doi Suthep is located up on the mountain, 3,520 feet above sea level and about 15 km. from Chiang Mai City. The Temple is approached on foot by climbing a steep Naga staircase comprising 290 steps, take time for me to reach the top :) The temple's pagoda contains holy Buddha relics, and attracts Buddhist pilgrims

www.virtualtourist.com

experience design 1.1

Another way to understand experiences is to identify the different media within which they occur. It's easiest, then, to identify the prominent attributes that differentiate products and media. There are no "right" answers here, and the differences in opinion and perception among people vary wildly. You might try discussing these in a group of people to gain an understanding about how media are viewed by others. This is an exercise I often use in classes and workshops, and the conclusions people make are some of the most valuable insights they will ever have.

Product Taxonomy

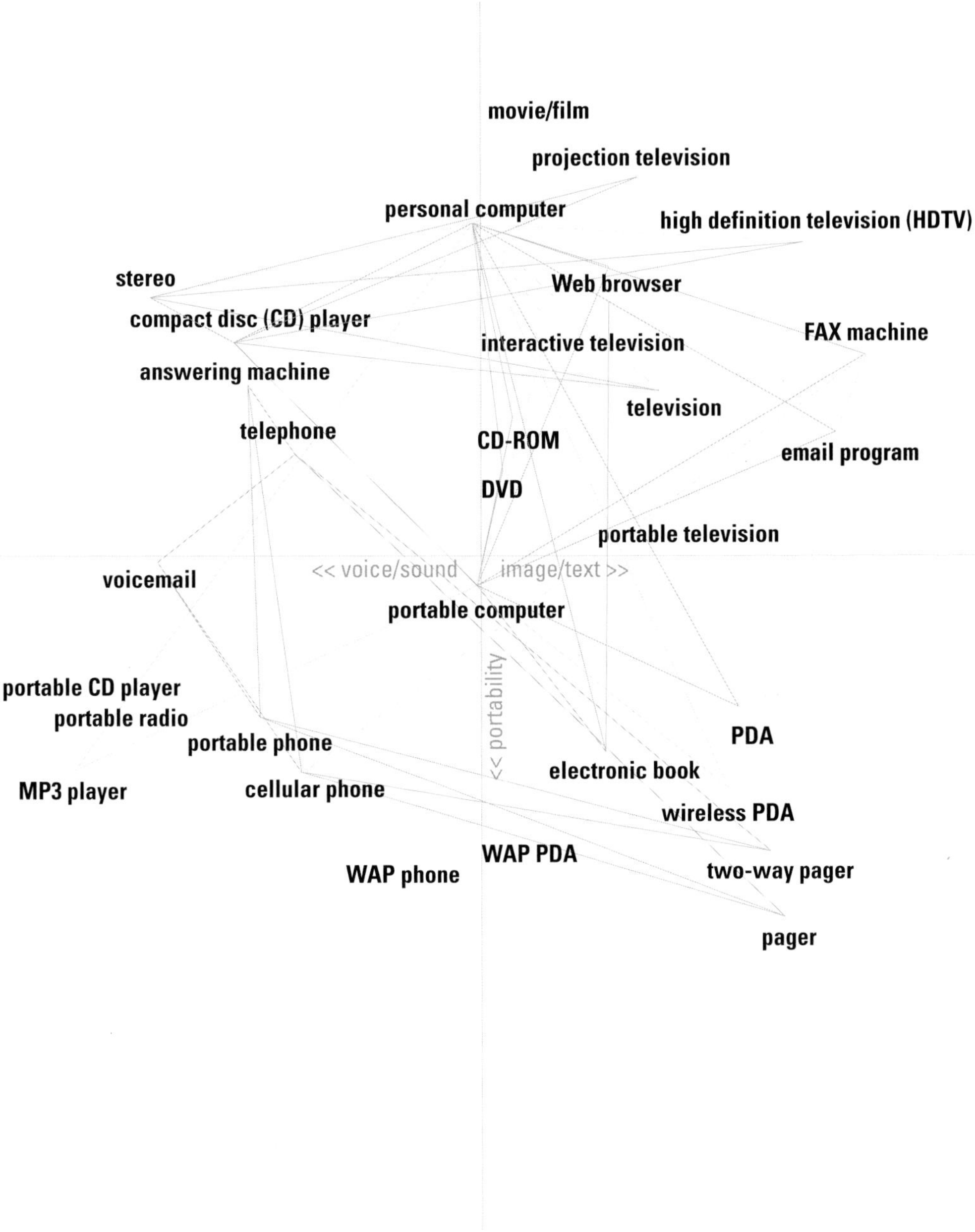

movie/film

projection television

personal computer

high definition television (HDTV)

stereo

Web browser

compact disc (CD) player

FAX machine

interactive television

answering machine

television

telephone

CD-ROM

email program

DVD

portable television

voicemail

<< voice/sound   image/text >>

portable computer

portable CD player

portable radio

PDA

portable phone

MP3 player

cellular phone

electronic book

wireless PDA

<< portability

WAP PDA

two-way pager

WAP phone

pager

Product Taxonomy

For a product that has been around for almost 30 years and has become such an important part of our daily life, automatic teller machines (ATMs) have evolved very little. The interfaces are still difficult for many people to use, though they do offer more options and, often, multiple languages now. Advertising within the screens have heightened our annoyance with them, while at the same time new functions have expanded our interactions (in Hong Kong, for example, some allow people to trade stocks).

Automated Teller Machines

ATMs have become so ubiquitous that when they aren't accessible, either through malfunction or availability (Tonga and Samoa, for example, had no ATMs as of 2000), we are unprepared for alternatives. In fact, travelers to other countries use them as an easy way to get money without having to interact with bank tellers in a foreign language. Compared to the experience they replace (waiting in line, filling-out forms, converting curriences, and speaking with a teller), these devices give us an enormous amount of new freedom. ATMs pop-up in places that are too small to have a bank branch, or where they can extend a bank's hours of operation, or where they can help us to purchase movie tickets or train fares. Where suspicion, fear, and unease were often associated with ATMs when they were first introduced (would they dispense the correct amount of money? would deposits actually get to our accounts? would we be able to correctly use the machine?), we now associate them with convenience.

photographs: Laurie Blavin   **Automated Teller Machines**

The Black Berry is the current wireless device-of-choice for wired (or unwired as this case may be) Internet enthusiasts and business people. The Black Berry is bigger than a pager but acts as a two-way communications device for text. It includes a small keyboard so people can enter text messages using two-thumbed typing, and it is always connected to a wireless paging service. The Black Berry is a pager, email system, personal organizer with schedule and address book, and notepad; and, it is compatible with sophisticated email servers already installed in many companies, including security protocols. This makes it an easily integrated solution for people on-the-move who mostly need email services and paging, and not a full computer.

Users of the Black Berry swear by its features and rave about its intuitive interface. For sure, it is easily learnable. Though not ubiquitous—mostly due to its relatively high cost—the Black Berry is growing in popularity because it does well exactly what it set out to do and never attempts to offer features that neither perform well for such small devices, or aren't essential for the needs of most users.

Black Berry

RIM 957 Wireless Handheld, launched in April 2000
www.blackberry.net

experience design 1.1

Black Berry

100 years, there will be no computers.
100 years, MPEG and QuickTime will be forgotten.
100 years, CD-ROMs will not exist (whether quad-speed or even faster).
100 years, there will be no Basic, C++, Perl, or HTML.
100 years, Mighty Morphin Power Rangers will (thankfully) be only a memo
100 years, RISC chips will be extinct.
100 years, there will be no PowerBooks.
100 years, Windows® will not exist (Bob® should be gone in less than 5).
100 years, DOS will still be around somewhere.
100 years, there will be no Mosaic, Netscape, CompuServe, Prodigy, or Amer
line.
100 years, Barney will be extinct.
100 years, set-top boxes, ITV, and HDTV will be forgotten.

s not that these things aren't important to somebody, but they should not
portant to you. These should not be foremost in your thoughts. However...

100 years, Dr. Seuss will still excite both kids and adults.
100 years, people will still buy, sell, and trade things that are important to th
100 years, spirituality will still help people guide their lives.
100 years, sex will still hold its allure, excitement, suspicion, and danger.
100 years, there will still be intolerance, hatred, bigotry, and greed.
100 years, conversations will still illuminate, enrage, engage, and inspire.
100 years, creativity will be even more important.
100 years, art will still be revered.
100 years, AT&T will still be here.
100 years, people will still throw dinner parties,
100 years, travelers will still explore the world.
100 years, there will still be holes in the ozone layer.
100 years, people will still wait in lines.
100 years, some people will still find sports fascinating.

One way of measuring experiences is to qualify them against personal value. This is intentionally vague because there is such a wide variety of meanings that people can associate with things. Research can explore which experiences people will spend the most time with and for which they would pay the most money—especially for new technologies or experiences. Since we can't look ahead in time for a comparison to future experiences, we need to look back. And we often need to look back over a time period that's long enough to give us some perspective, **like 100 years.**

100 Years

Experiences throughout history can inform the design of experiences today and in the future. Professor Marcello Truzzi

This looking back over our shoulder is critical because most technological industries have almost-nonexistent attention spans and proclaim it worthless to look ahead more than six months. This short-sightedness is one of the reasons the industry is so hit-and-miss, having soaring successes as well as spectacular failures—and many more failures than successes. Looking back and understanding people in a longer, broader context allows us to find more universal aspects of **human values** that we can tap into for designing more successful experiences. This is an approach that doesn't always work for fads but is valuable for products and experiences that hope to have more longevity and a greater impact.

100 Years

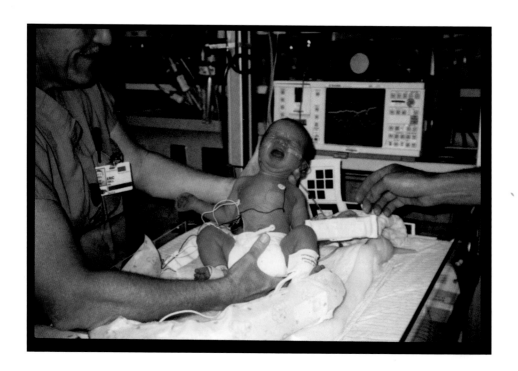

The two quintessential and ubiquitous experiences of one's life are birth and death. Their constancy make them experiences worth studying—all the more so since they're so emotionally charged. Our feelings about these experiences vary greatly from culture to culture and change substantially as we age. While some people are perpetually trying to avoid death, others embrace it as a natural and necessary part of life. Psychologists attribute many of our emotional problems to our inabilities to deal with birth and death issues, our own mortality, and the deaths and births of those around us.

Birth

Both birth and death are experiences that have much to teach us—about design, about life, about our psyches, and about ourselves. Mostly, our views haven't changed substantially over the years and centuries, at least within our faiths and cultures, and they provide a set of values upon which to base new experiences.

photographs: Laurie Blavin   **Death**

Matchmaking is an activity as old as history itself. In fact, the history of finding a partner or spouse tells a great deal about a culture. In many traditional cultures, matches were made by a third-party or by parents. In Western cultures, and increasingly elsewhere in the world, people now make their own decisions about whom to marry or, at least, spend their lives with. With the divorce rate as high as it is, it's unclear which method yields better, or more lasting, results.

Long a mainstay of the online world, dating sites have promised to streamline the process of finding a compatible partner. However, finding the right person for you is more difficult than simply matching criteria, interests, and ages. The plethora of online dating sites is a testament to the difficulty in setting the context and connecting two people. This is the reason for new online services that not only attempt to match

Chemistry.com

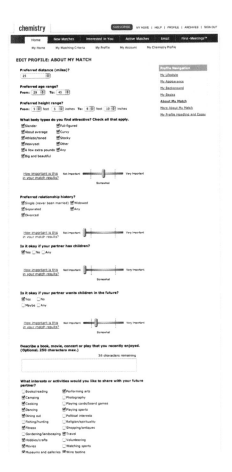

preferences but also match personalities. They use more sophisticated models (and ask more questions) to better place people in a personality or behavioral context.

Chemistry.com is one example of this approach. You don't simple join, upload a photo, write a description, and check a lot of boxes (though you do those as well). Specific questionnaires analyze answers according to "scientific" behavioral models. In some cases, people with like personalities should be put together. In others, they should be complemented with dissimilar personalities.

In addition to using, often, proprietary behavioral models, they offer expanded services to guide the process of introducing people and manage the interaction at the start, much like an executive recruiter might place someone into the perfect job at the right company.

Chemistry.com

In his novel, *Generation X: Tales for an Accelerated Culture*, author Douglas Coupland describes a "takeaway" as "that one memory of Earth that you'll take away with you when you die that proves that you were alive."

Takeaways are another exercise that helps us derive meaning from the things we experience. Ponder for a moment what memories you have that might qualify as a takeaway. Perhaps you don't have one yet, but you probably have an idea as to what it might be. Think about what is important to you in your life. What will you remember? What makes your life worth living?

It's likely that your takeaway doesn't involve technology—few people's do. Most likely, it doesn't involve media like TV or radio either. It just may be that technological experiences are sufficiently mediated so that they become less direct and, therefore, more difficult to become important. Perhaps it's because technological and media experiences are so often reproduced, their rarity or specialness is lessened.

In any case, it's useful to deconstruct the meaning of these important experiences in order to understand why they are so important to us. In fact, these attributes are some of the most important we can discover and, hopefully, reproduce in the experiences we create for others. Transformative experiences, those that help people change in some way that is important to them, are typically good for measuring value.

Some of the attributes we have uncovered appear on the following pages—especially those in the Interaction Design section. However, these are only the tip of the experiential iceberg. It is up to you to discover and explore more.

Takeaways

Generation X: Tales for an Accelerated Culture
isbn: 031205436X
www.coupland.com

setting is a poolside in a run-down Palm Springs [apar]tment complex where a few twenty-something friends [a]nd tell stories to each other.

[Let] me see your eyes."

[Claire] leans over to allow Elvissa to put a hand around his ... and extract information from his eyes, the blue color [of] Dutch souvenir plates. She takes an awfully long time [We]ll, okay. Maybe you're not all that bad. I might even tell [you] a special story in a few minutes. Remind me. But it [dep]ends. I want you to tell me something first, after you're [dea]d and buried and floating around whatever place we go [w]hat's going to be your best memory of earth?"

[Wh]at do you mean? I don't get it."

... at one moment for you to [de]scribe what it's like to be alive [on this] planet. What's your takeaway?"

[Clai]re is silence. Tobias doesn't get her point, and frankly, [neither do I. She] continues. "Fake yuppie experiences that [you'll] spend money on, like white water rafting or [...]land don't count. I want to hear some [...] moment [of] your life that proves you're really alive."

[Tobi]as does not readily volunteer any info. I think he needs [...] first.

[I've] got one," says Claire. All eyes turn to her.

[Sno]w," she says to us. At the very moment a hailstorm of [...] cranks upward from the brown silk soil of the Arthurs' yard next door...

I always remember the first time I saw snow. I was [...]ve and it was just after the first and biggest divorce. I [was] in New York visiting my mother and was standing [on a] traffic island in the middle of Park Avenue. I'd [never] been out of L.A. before. I was entranced by the big [...] looking up at the Pan Am Building and [conte]mplating the essential problem of Manhattan."

[Whi]ch being?' I ask.

[Which i]s that there's too much weight improperly [distributed]: towers and elevators; steel, stone, and cement. [Piled] mass up so high that gravity itself could end up [getting] warped--some dreadful inversion--an exchange [of land] with the sky." (I love it when Claire gets weird.) "I [was] gagging at the thought of this. But right then my [moth]er yanked at my sleeve because the walk signal [was] green. And when I turned my head to walk across, [I] ce went bang.

[...] into my first snowflake ever. It melted in my eye. I [didn't] even know what it was at first, but then I saw millions [of flak]es--all white and smelling like ozone, floating [down]ward like the shed skin of angels. Even Allan stopped. [Traf]fic was honking at us, but time stood still. And so, yes-- [my t]ake one memory of earth away with me, that moment [will] be the one. To this day I consider my right eye charmed."

[Nice] says Elvissa. She turns to Tobias. "Get the drift?"

[Let] me think a second."

[I've] got one," says Dag with some enthusiasm, partially [to wit], I suspect, of wanting to score brownie points [with] Elvissa. "It happened in 1974. In

[King]ston, Ontario." He lights a cigarette and we wait. "My [frie]nd and I were at a gas station and I was given the task of [filling] up the gas tank--a Galaxy 500, snazzy car. And filling [it] was a big responsibility for me. I was one of those [...] kids who always got colds and never got the hang of

shit. I felt so small. But instead he smiled and said to me, "Hey, Sport. Isn't the smell of gasoline great? Close your eyes and inhale. So clean. It smells like the future."

"Well, with that, I closed my eyes just as he asked, and breathed in deeply. And at that point I saw the bright orange light of the sun coming through my eyelids, smelled the gasoline and my knees buckled. Both was the most perfect moment of my life, and so if you ask me (and I have a lot hopes pinned on this), heaven just has to be an awful lot like those few seconds. That's my memory of earth."

"Was it leaded or unleaded?" asks Tobias.

"Leaded," replies Dag.

"Perfect."

Tobias can barely contain himself. His body is poised forward, like a child in a shopping cart waiting to unload the presweetened breakfast cereals: "I know what my memory is! I know what it is now!"

"Well just tell us then," says Elvissa.

"It's like this--" (God only knows what it will be) "Every summer back in Tacoma Park" (Washington, DC) "there was an eastern city) "my dad and I would rig up a shortwave radio that he had leftover from 1950s. We'd string a wire across the yard at sunset and tether it up to the linden tree to act as an antenna.

We'd try all of the bands, and if the radiation in the Van Allen belt was low, then we'd pick up just about everywhere: Johannesburg, Radio Moscow, Japan, Punjabi stuff. But more than anything we'd get signals from South America, these weird haunted-sounding bolero-samba transmissions from dinner theaters in Ecuador and Caracas and Rio. The music would come in faintly--faintly but clearly.

"One night Mom came out onto the patio in a sundress and carrying a glass pitcher of lemonade. Dad swept her into his arms and they danced to the samba music with Mom still holding the pitcher. She was squealing but loving it. I think she was enjoying that little bit of danger the threat broken glass added to the dancing. And there were crickets cricking and the transformer humming on the power line behind the garage and I had my suddenly young parents all to myself--them and this faint music that sounded like heaven--faraway, clear, and impossible to contact--coming from this faceless place that was always summer and where beautiful people were always dancing and where it was impossible to call by telephone, even if you wanted to. Now that's earth to me."

Well, who'd have thought Tobias was capable of such thoughts? We're going to have to do a reevaluation of this lad.

"Andy?" Elvissa looks to me. "You?"

"I know my earth memory. It's a smell--the smell of bacon. It was a Sunday morning at home and we were all having breakfast, an unprecedented occurrence since me and a six of my brothers and sisters inherited my mother's tendency to detest the sight of food in the morning. We'd sleep in instead.

"Anyhow, there wasn't even a special reason for the meal. All nine of us simply ended up in the kitchen by accident, with everyone being funny and nice to each other, and reading out the grisly bits from the newspaper. It was sunny no one was being psycho or mean.

"I remember very clearly standing by the stove and frying

Takeaways

Unfortunately, I only have a handful of candidates for "takeaways." The memories most important and wondrous to me are few, but I will share one…

Driving back to our rooms in a calm, pitch-black night in Costa Rica, my friends and I pulled-off to the side of the road to talk. We were in the middle of trees and fields on the edge of a jungle. At first, no one even paid attention to the absolute darkness and still silence that surrounded our truck, but slowly we lost our will to continue speaking as our eyes adjusted to the dark and the jungle came alive with the light of thousands of fireflies.

Fireflies

We were speechless as we watched their visual mating signals from a hundred yards a way to right in front of us on our windshield. The twinkling lights from the fireflies were as much like a field of stars, as a field of fireflies were like a field of fairies. It was a magical, unexpected moment and a reminder of how stunning nature can be when you take the time to look. It was also a timeless moment—not that I wasn't aware of time passing, but because it felt like it could go on forever, without end.

Fireflies

oday my house fell into the water.
he pacific ocean.

he last month has been saturated with persistent
ains and insistent waves and northern california
eems to be prepping for the apocalypse. the rains
ad been degrading our cliff and we would watch daily
s different elements of the thing would deteriorate
nd drop, school busses in size, sub-audio plops
nto the beach some 70 feet below our back porch.

--

 went to karate at 8. i got back at 9:30. it was
arm and i opened the door to let some of the rare
unlight- in the garage my cats interpreting as i
oved boxes around and i heard a noise on the side
f the house like someone kicking something and i
hought it impossible that there was someone there
nd i opened the door to look at the ocean.. the
liff was breaking away so fast, deep, and moving
oward me like a huge anti-matter snake and the
irt was falling away like there was someone under-
eath pulling at it like a carpet. the ground was
alling out from under the house.

tood there as the cliff slid toward me 6 feet in
alf that many seconds, like an invisible predator,
nough to convince me it was time to move more than
y eyebrows. grabbed cats. jumped out garage door.
isa was in the living room. talking on the phone...
 told her to get out of the house. she did. and
e waited in the front yard and listened and waited
nd wondered and the wind blew a bit and we heard the
cean and the world seemed very still and blue.

0 minutes passed. we heard a thud, or so it seemed.

he razorbladeopportunity to really part with
veruthing: have uou ever been pushed away and as uou

boar.com/days/collapse

designer/writer/photographer:
Mark Meadows
images: copyright 1999 Mark Meadows

experience design 1.1

```
2479 Feb 23 23:29 house_collapse.html
```

eb 24 1998, some pictures   some i took.

```
12180 Feb 26 08:48 cnn_snap.jpg
32035 Feb 24 20:44 lisa01.jpg
69025 Feb 24 21:53 pix02.jpg
62276 Feb 24 21:55 pix03.jpg
90512 Feb 24 21:56 pix04.jpg
50197 Feb 24 21:52 pix05.jpg
41335 Feb 24 21:53 pix06.jpg
47433 Feb 24 20:46 duo.jpg
```

eb 25 1998, newspaper clips.

```
245267 Feb 24 20:53 chronicle_cover.jpg
105873 Feb 24 20:54 examiner_cover.jpg
192905 Feb 24 20:53 chronicle_cover_detail.jpg
```

eb 25 1998, phone call from a friend.

```
707186 Feb 24 20:25 marko.wav
```

Sometimes an event can leave a lasting impression—especially a personal catastrophe. When Mark Meadow's house slid into the sea, it changed his thinking about what a home is. He chronicles here what he and his girlfriend went through in the days prior to losing his home.

boar.com/days/collapse

experience design 1.1

Information design has only recently been identified as a discipline; it is one in which we all participate and, in some way, we always have. Information is really data transformed into something more valuable by building context around it so that it becomes understandable.

One of the first things we can learn about understanding is that it is a continuum from Data, a somewhat raw ingredient, to Wisdom, an ultimate achievement. Along this spectrum is an ever-increasing value chain of understanding, which is derived from an increasing level of context and meaning that becomes more personal and more sophisticated—not to mention more valuable—as it approaches Wisdom.

There are many ways to describe this spectrum. In *The Experience Economy,* H. Joseph Pine II and James H. Gilmore equate this spectrum with the following parts:

Noise	=	Commodities:	Value is for raw materials.
Data	=	Products:	Value is for tangible things.
Information	=	Services:	Value is for activities.
Knowledge	=	Experiences:	Value is the time customers spend with you.
Wisdom	=	Transformations:	Value is the demonstrated outcome the customer achieves.

An alternate explanation for this last category might be that "Transformations" is really "Meaning" and that this level of experience is important—and more valuable—because it evokes so much meaning. This is explored in detail in *Making Meaning* and *Experience Design 2.*

We have learned from information design that structure, itself, has meaning

and that it can affect not only the effectiveness but the meaning of a message. This axiom has been proven time and time again in the presentation of "statistics" and in their "interpretation." People readily agree and believe that statistics can "lie." For years, Richard Saul Wurman has shown us that simply reorganizing the same pieces in different ways changes our understanding of them, as well as the whole. A quick survey in any medium shows a notable lack of innovation in most products of communication in terms of their structure and form. This is mostly due to a lack of initiative and imagination rather than a lack of ability or opportunity. To build more effective communications, we must experiment much more with the form these might take.

The term **information overload** has been used for several decades now but I don't think that this is really the problem. Instead, consider Richard Saul Wurman's definition of **information anxiety**. In his latest book, *Information Anxiety 2,* he and I define this malady in terms of its social effect: a lack of context and meaning in our world. It isn't so much

Information Design

that there's more to read (although this is certainly the case), but that there is such a paucity of valuable insights and meaning; no one has shown that there is, in fact, any greater number of meanings to understand than ever before.

The way to lessen this condition is to create more insight, perhaps the most valuable product of all

Insight is what is created as we add context and give care to both the presentation and organization of data as well as the particular needs of our audience. And as insight is increased by building with more care and context, communication is pushed higher up or deeper into the understanding chain.

In the following pages, you'll see examples of all of these concepts, including multiple ways of organizing data and the emotional impact it can have on the message. Information presentations often can be seductive, sometimes in the content, often in visual presentation, but most important is their form and ability to communicate clearly.

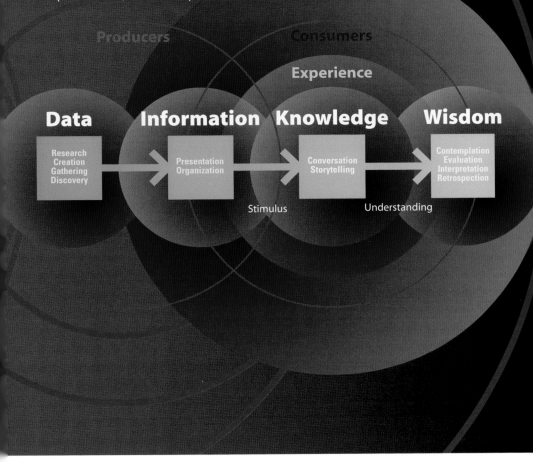

The Experience Economy, Joseph Pine II and James H. Gilmore, isbn: 0875848192
Information Anxiety 2, Richard Saul Wurman, isbn: 0789724103

Information Design

Data is not information.

This is paramount to realize. Though we use the two terms interchangeably in our culture—mostly to glorify data that has no right to be ennobled—they mean distinctly different things.

Data is raw and often overabundant. While it may have meaning to experts, it is, for the most part, only the building blocks on which relevance is built. It also should never be produced for delivery in raw form to an audience—especially a consumer audience. This isn't so that it can be kept secret but because it has no inherent value. Until it is transformed into information (with context), its meaning is of little value and only contributes to the anxiety we feel dealing with so much information in our lives.

An unfortunate fallacy we live under is that this is an "Age of Information."

Never before has so much data been produced. Yet our lives are not enhanced by any of it. Worse, this situation will only become more pervasive.

Data is often passed off as information, while the bulk of it doesn't even qualify. For example, CNN used to fill the space between advertising and news on its television channels with "factoids"—probably the best word yet to ensure that there isn't any meaning, information, or value attached to it. These serve not to inform, but to create the perception of information. Each is a wasted opportunity for actually enlightening us with insightful observations about the news around us. Instead, they serve only as worthless trivia that mostly divert our attention from more important things, while giving the illusion that accuracy and obscurity are replacements for understanding.

Data

Likewise, titles like Chief Information Officer (CIO) and even Information Technology (IT) further mask the problem. In most cases, neither has anything to do with information, communication, or any systems for generating these. Rather they are merely steeped in data, data systems, data technologies, and data processes. The famed "productivity paradox" (the lack of proof that any gains in increased productivity stem from computers and related technologies) is mostly a crisis arising from this misunderstanding of data and information. What we tend to measure is only data and while this has increased in our society, it has not—and cannot—improve productivity or anything else because it lacks the value to do so, or the value to make meaningful change. Once we re-educate ourselves as to what information really is, then we may be able to find the opportunities for increased understanding and productivity.

Data is so uninforming that we can liken it to heavy-winter clothing, enshrouding us as we interact with each other. It doesn't completely stop us from communicating, but it makes it much more difficult, and it surely makes any complex interactions more laborious.

Data

have been one of the few commonly accepted forms of data in our lives that have garnered

respect. This is beginning to change w

presentations of market information (such as the *Map of the Market* on page 94).

raw as can be imagined, yet it still holds a lot of

Without knowing a great deal about the market (common measures such as volumes, volatili

performance is difficult, if not impossible, without contex

Stock Ticker

Raw data is easy to find in our world—but useful data is more rare. Stock tickers

ew technologies that offer easier tracking tools (filtering only the stocks that interest us), and richer

The data streaming off the archetypal ticker is about as

espect in both the professional investment world and among amateur investors.

verage prices, political climate, etc.), trying to interpret any great meaning in a particular stock's

et we still publish this data everyday in newspapers.

Stock Ticker

This is one of those experiences that never could have existed before the Web. J-track enables anyone to view the tracking data for all the satellites in orbit around the Earth—at least the ones that NASA tracks. There is no meaning or evaluation provided, nor synopsis or knowledge, but the novel nature of the data itself—certainly for those of us outside the aerospace industry—is a rare glimpse into a phenomenon that we can barely perceive otherwise.

J-Track

science.nasa.gov/Realtime/JTrack/Spacecraft.html

xperience design 1.1

0

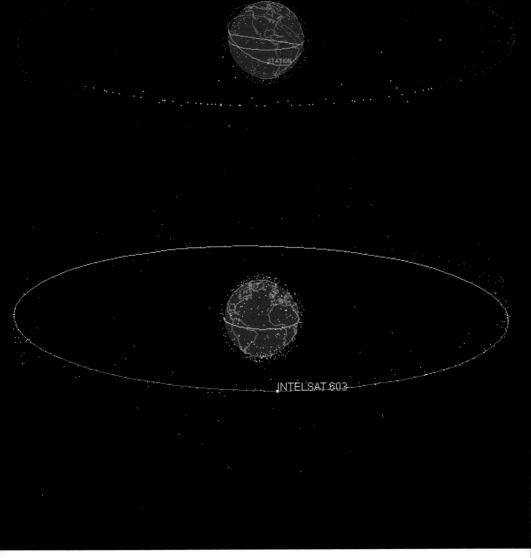

principal designers: Patrick Meyer, Tim Hervath, and Becky Bray

J-Track

Information is the beginning of meaning

Information is data put into context with thought given to its organization and presentation. And even at that, it is only the lowest form of meaning as the context involved in creating and presenting data is usually basically generalized. However, at least there *is* context, unlike data.

Because information is so basic, it tends to be formal and rather impersonal. Also, most of us have such poor information skills—that is, the skills necessary for reorganizing, analyzing, synthesizing, and presenting data—information tends to be even less sophisticated when it finally comes into being.

We all create information on some level, though most of us aren't consciously aware of doing so. However, we do make note of those people or sources that we tend to trust and understand better than others. We do feel a difference when we feel we're being understood, and a frustration when we aren't. Because information is part of our lives, we all are both producers and consumers. This is why it is so critical for us to have basic information skills. Without these skills we relinquish the responsibility and the ability to create information for ourselves and those around us—to add value, if for no other purpose than to relate our own personal stories and experiences.

Like data, information can be captured and frozen in time. It can be printed in books or inherent in natural phenomena (like tides). However, it is only of value if we know how to decode it, if we can speak the language with which it has been encoded, and if the information hasn't been obscured by other phenomena.

Unfortunately, there are very few products that help us create information. Software manufacturers, in particular, have been adept at creating tools that allow us to manipulate data, color and animate it, but not help us create meaning from it. Usually, these tools only make things worse as their effects only mask meaning further.

Organizing Things

The organization and presentation of data can profoundly change its understanding. Presentation can affect the knowledge people build and the experience people have. This is where information design can have its greatest impact. It is the discipline concerned with transforming data into information by creating context and structure. Information design is the method through which graphic design and other visual disciplines are expressed.

Though data organization is a profoundly important process, it isn't necessarily a foreboding one. As Richard Saul Wurman has so often shown, there are only a few ways to organize data in order to create information. In fact, it is often a fun exercise that yields surprising and satisfying results. Meaning is formed by the arrangement of data and transformed as we restructure it.

Information

Consider the basic ways we can organize data, being mindful that organization and presentation are different concepts. Data can only be organized within a few principles: **Magnitude, Time, Numbers, Alphabet, Category, Location,** and **Randomness.**

Magnitude, Time, Number, and Alphabet are all sequences of some type, which we can use to organize things based on a similar characteristic shared by all the data. The last three of these attributes (**Time, Number,** and **Alphabet**) are special, simple sequences that we've come to understand through training but which often have no inherent meaning for the data. These organizational structures are merely easy for us to use, even though their use can seem somewhat artificial.

Category and **Location** are organizations that also use some inherently meaningful aspect of the data around which the data can be oriented. Because these organizations are more qualitative than quantitative, they often seem more "natural" and less artificial. These two organizations can be thought of as two-dimensional (and sometimes even three-dimensional) in that they each orient data, necessarily, in at least two directions (whereas sequences like those above are fundamentally one-dimensional). There is no greater value in data arranged one-, two- or three-dimensionally as it is meaningful. However, 2D data arrangements can tend to offer more accessibility since there is more than one way to access the inforrmation (either dimension).

Randomness is the lack of organization. It is often important when we're trying to build an experience that isn't necessarily easy (a perfectly legitimate endeavor as long as it's appropriate), for example, as in a game.

The same organization (for instance a geographical or locational one) can be presented or *expressed* in several different forms, e.g., maps, written descriptions and directions, illustrated in graphs, charts, and timelines, or read to us audibly. The organization need not change through all of these forms and, thus, the meaning won't either. However, the presentation will still affect a person's ability to understand.

Data often has its own natural organization. It almost has a *will* to be organized in a particular way (still within one of the forms we've discussed). Experimenting with different organizations is often a process of uncovering the organization that exudes from the data, thereby informing its structure.

Each organization creates a new mental model of the data and can lead to new understandings of the data. These can sometimes revolutionize our understanding of even familiar subjects since they illuminate an aspect that might have been confusing or obscured before.

"Information is data endowed with relevance and purpose."
 Peter Drucker

Information

Traffic signs are so common that we rarely stop to consider how effective they are in alerting us to dangers or directing us to our destinations. The context is what makes these signs effective, as well as the training we receive when we reach driving age. Additionally, the effectiveness of these signs relies upon the convention of using them, and the shared agreement about their meaning.

Traffic Signs

Traffic Signs

The transformation of information usually yields more information, and sometimes more than the original information itself.

Google's Translator isn't the first online translation service but it is one of the most popular. The perennial dream of computer developers and users to help us better understand each other, despite language difficulties, is growing closer to realization, though it doesn't often seem that way when you use a translator for a specific sentence. Language is notoriously complex and irregular and translations must function at multiple levels (not just words, but syntax, semantics, context, and take into account slang as well). While the Google translation isn't as accurate as that completed by a human, native-speaker of the translated language, it is reasonable and certainly good enough for casual correspondence. At the very least, it's usually better than no translation at all.

The information inherent in the original message leads to new information in the translation, but introduces two kinds of other information: The first is what might be termed the "mis-translation" or unintended meaning; the second is the experience we get comparing the two messages—even casually—and the familiarization and exposure we have to the translation.

Google is continuously refining its tools (as are others) and they've recently added new languages, including Asian languages, such as Chinese and Korean. This is a particularly amazing trick as many of these languages use different character sets and entirely different syntax (sentence structure).

Over time, our ability to community with others in different languages may open new possibilities to share knowledge and create bonds that, otherwise, would have been impossible.

Google has always shown a democratic and egalitarian approach to languages (a topic that can easily become contentious and elitist). While the translator doesn't yet work in every language (this is one of the most difficult feats we've attempted with computers, mind you), Google has long allowed people to use its search interface in a wide variety of languages, including smaller communities like Esperanto and Klingon (there are more speakers of the latter than the former now) and some silly instances, like Elmer Fudd.

Google Translator

www.google.com/language_tools

Afrikaans | Hebrew | Punjabi
Albanian | Hindi | Quechua
Amharic | Hungarian | Romanian
Arabic | Icelandic | Romansh
Armenian | Indonesian | Russian
Azerbaijani | Interlingua | Scots Gaelic
Basque | Irish | Serbian
Belarusian | Italian | Serbo-Croatian
Bengali | Japanese | Sesotho
Bihari | Javanese | Shona
Bork, bork, bork! | Kannada | Sindhi
Bosnian | Kazakh | Sinhalese
Breton | Klingon | Slovak
Bulgarian | Korean | Slovenian
Cambodian | Kurdish | Somali
Catalan | Kyrgyz | Spanish
Chinese (Simplified) | Laothian | Sundanese
Chinese (Traditional) | Latin | Swahili
Corsican | Latvian | Swedish
Croatian | Lingala | Tajik
Czech | Lithuanian | Tamil
Danish | Macedonian | Tatar
Dutch | Malay | Telugu
Elmer Fudd | Malayalam | Thai
English | Maltese | Tigrinya
Esperanto | Marathi | Tonga
Estonian | Moldavian | Turkish
Faroese | Mongolian | Turkmen
Filipino | Nepali | Twi
Finnish | Norwegian | Uighur
French | Norwegian (Nynorsk) | Ukrainian
Frisian | Occitan | Urdu
Galician | Oriya | Uzbek
Georgian | Pashto | Vietnamese
German | Persian | Welsh
Greek | Pig Latin | Xhosa
Guarani | Polish | Yiddish
Gujarati | Portuguese (Brazil) | Yoruba
Hacker | Portuguese (Portugal) | Zulu

Google Translator

experience design 1.1

The difference between information and knowledge is a difficult one to explain. Knowledge isn't just a more complex version of information—its use is different as well. Knowledge is a kind of meta-information that must be understood in a more general way. In fact, **a definition of knowledge could be "sufficiently generalized solutions gained through experience."** This means that knowledge is something that is, necessarily, accessible in many and varied contexts and situations, and not merely descriptive of details in particular ones.

This generalization is important because it makes knowledge more useful, and it helps distinguish knowledge from information since its meaning must be distilled from information in order to be understood as knowledge. In other words, **generalization is a criteria that helps us understand a meaning that is deeper or of a higher-order than information.** This is also possible only through experience since we cannot distinguish knowledge from information unless we can compare its use in several, different situations, each of which is an experience.

While we can help build knowledge for others (in pointing it out as well as designing the experiences to make it easier to understand), this is the beginning of the crossing of a threshold in which **people must build these kinds of understandings for themselves.** Wisdom, for example, is something people can only build for themselves and knowledge shares part of this characteristic.

Knowledge is increasingly personal in that the processes
in our minds that help define and understand knowledge rely increasingly on personal contexts, content, and previous understandings, and less on shared ones. By the time we can build wisdom, the context is so personal that we are unable to share it easily. This process of internalization helps create knowledge and wisdom but at the same time makes it more difficult to share.

Context moves from the global (societal or cultural) to the local (shared among increasingly smaller groups and more idiosyncratic) to the personal (easily understood only to ourselves without explanation). **Knowledge, then, becomes more casual in its use. As it becomes more personal,** it cannot be used as formally with others; and formal situations often can make it more difficult to communicate knowledge.

Knowledge also builds upon itself, making it increasingly easier to acquire more knowledge.

This is because it helps us use and organize our own contexts and understandings, and these structures help us more easily integrate new experiences, information, data, and, thus, knowledge into this system. The practice also gives us confidence and decreases fear about learning and understanding.

Because the experience is so critical to building knowledge, the richer the experience, the more likely it is to fit one of our contextual models and the more able we are to find meaning in it. However, just because it is rich, doesn't mean it is effective. Often, rich experiences offer only more stimulation and not more context. This stimulation can just

Knowledge

as easily make it more difficult to decode and integrate any knowledge as make it more likely. This is why activities like storytelling and conversation are so powerful and necessary for creating knowledge. **They allow us to interact with the information in a way that helps us build personal context and integrate the information into our previous understandings.** Any valuable education or learning, therefore, cannot exist without building these processes into its models.

Knowledge

Of course, there are many kinds of classes, but cooking classes are particularly exciting since the skills they teach are applicable to everyday life. The products created are also delicious and are something in which most people can take pride. Every class is an opportunity to impart knowledge. Cooking classes make this easier since most allow students to cook themselves, and it is this experience that allows for knowledge to transfer more readily.

Cooking Class

Actually performing an activity is almost always more memorable than simply watching. Because our whole body is involved in the activity, our kinetic, olfactory, and tactile memory is stimulated in addition to our visual and sonic memory. This creates a richer experience and binds our memories together, often in subconscious ways.

Cooking Class

Langwidget is an ingenious Web-based translation tool that mixes machine and human translation techniques to create more accurate, repeatable, and learnable translations based on the knowledge and experience of human translators. In addition, the translation engine and rules get better over time with more use and more exposure to human translators.

Until langwidget, past solutions have tried to use computers for brute-force machine translation (delivering incredibly fast and incredibly poor translation) or used human translators to assist machine translation with fuzzy-matching techniques. However, langwidget's approach is to learn, standardize, and share human-built translations by watching translators work (leveraging their more adept experience and knowlege) and then sharing these "rules" through the system automatically with every other translator. The system automatically learns, shares, and ranks solutions as "rules" without translators needing to define them. This matchingcan be at the sentence, word, punctuation, or rule level. Once in the system, they're automatically available and shown to everyone else in the system, whenthe context is appropriate. The more the system is used, the more rules in the database, and the more automatic suggestions available to everyone.

In addition, the system ranks rules by popularity so it learns which translations are most preferred, in context, and reorders them based on preference. This allows langwidget to use statistical analysis to better present options and, in the future, use both rules and statistics to automatically translate whole texts with much better accuracy and relevance. It also gives the tool the ability to parse deeply complex texts easily with much better results.

langwidget

Creator: Jed Schmidt

www.langwidget.com

langwidget

ALPHA

File   View   Tools   Help

おはようございます、
シェドロフさん！

おはようございます、
おはようございます
§ Good morning
さん！

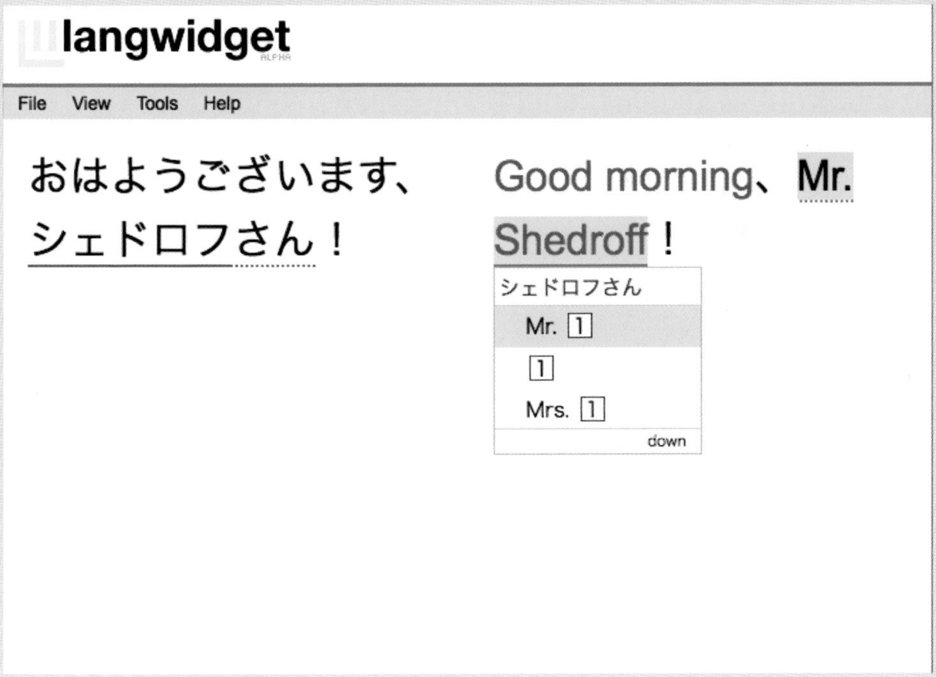

---

langwidget

ALPHA

File   View   Tools   Help

おはようございます、
シェドロフさん！

Good morning、 Mr.
Shedroff ！

シェドロフさん	
Mr.	1
	1
Mrs.	1
	down

Wisdom is even more difficult to explain than knowledge since the levels of context become even more personal, and thus the higher-level nature of wisdom renders it much more obscure. Where knowledge is mainly sufficiently generalized solutions, **think of wisdom as "sufficiently generalized approaches and values that can be applied in many, varied situations."**

Wisdom cannot be created like data and information, and it cannot be shared with others like knowledge. Because the context is so personal it becomes almost exclusive to our own minds, and incompatible with the minds of others without extensive translation. This translation requires not only a base of knowledge and the opportunities for experiences that help create wisdom, but also the processes of introspection, retrospection, interpretation, and contemplation.

We can value wisdom in others but only we can create it for ourselves.

Because of this, it doesn't come naturally or accidentally; it is for the most part created deliberately. Exposing people, especially children, to wisdom and the concept of wisdom is critical in opening the door to becoming wise (or having common sense); however, the work cannot be done for us by others. It can only be done by ourselves and this requires an intimate understanding and relationship with ourselves.

It is quite possible that the path to wisdom is not even open until we approach understanding with an openness and tolerance for ambiguity. Fear and rigid tenets often create barriers to truly understanding experiences and situations and creating wisdom from them. This doesn't mean that we must be without principles, but that we must be constantly willing and open to challenging our principles and modifying them—even abandoning them—in the face of new experiences that prove more reliable or illuminating. Since wisdom is so personal, a fear or lack of understanding about yourself becomes one of the most extreme roadblocks to becoming wise. Since we are always striving to better understand ourselves, this becomes a continuous process that requires that we constantly evaluate ourselves as well as our previous understandings and functions.

Wisdom

Wisdom

Dinner parties are hardly new experiences—they still satisfy our needs for entertainment, food, and company. This is especially true for Mary Jordan's annual fete honoring her experiences in Burma. The 80 or so invitees in 2000 not only briought sake and donations for a 35-foot carved Buddha to be presented as a gift to the people of Burma next year, but specific contributions to the performances and entertainment of the dinner party guests were also required. These include probing questions to be answered (which are pulled at random from a bowl at Mary's whim), mysterious locations (also written on paper and relinquished to a different bowl), and appropriate (or approximate) dress to help make the experience special.

In addition to their own preparations, all guests are expected to perform and participate in the performance for others. Experience and performance are the operative themes here, and the pieces range from poetry readings to improvisation to music and dance to acts that defy description.

Guests are also made to perform rituals upon arrival, some of which include cleansing their thoughts and minds, fording streams, and submitting to a sonic massage by dijeridoo.

The wisdom of the rituals and preparations is that people need to purposefully and deliberately cross the boundary from the outside world to the inside world created for the party. The rituals and performances subtly guide guests to contemplate the thoughts and offerings made by their fellow guests, consider their values and reactions to these experiences, and challenge their current beliefs in light of new knowledge.

Burmese Tea Party

www.virtualtourist.com

creator: Mary Jordan
held annually since 1998

Burmese Tea Party

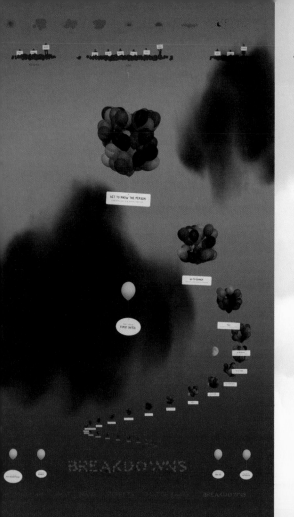

Online dating is always a challenging activity but rarely is it contemplative and poetic in the way that Jonathan Harris' and Seb Kamvar's commissioned piece for the Museum of Modern Art in New York. Far from a standard online dating system, *I Want You to Want Me* takes a different approach that assimilates and compares online ads in a way that prompts us to think about more than attributes and characteristics. *I Want You to Want Me* makes goals clear and deeper needs in an environment that supports exploration, introspection, and interpretation.

I Want You to Want Me

iwantyoutowantme.org

experience design 1.1

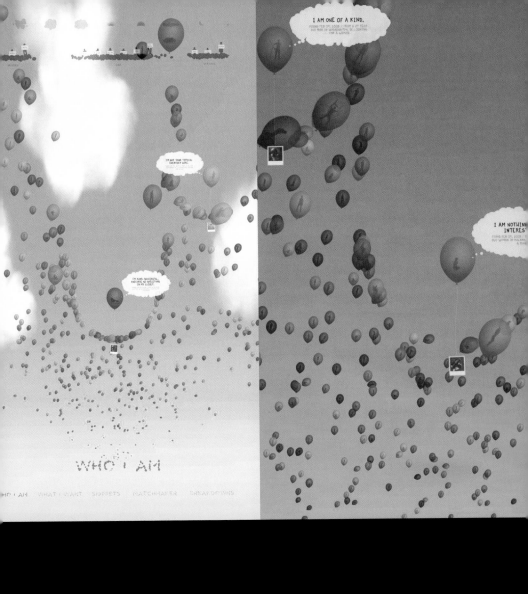

creators: Jonathan Harris and Sam Kamvar

I Want You to Want Me

The most important aspect of any design is how it is understood in the minds of the audience.

This concept, whether fully or partially formed, is a **cognitive model**. Everyone forms cognitive models for nearly everything they encounter—particularly those things they interact with repeatedly, or those things that we focus on because they are important to us. Some people are more adept at forming cognitive models than others, and these abilities also differ between people in their type of understanding—that is, some people form understandings textually, visually, aurally, temporally, geographically, and so forth. In any case, the form of the experience is what gives it meaning since this is what people experience directly.

Whether or not you focus on creating a cognitive model for your experience, your participants will nonetheless. They might form a mental map of the sequence or process or location. It might be of their feelings, or merely a randomly strung together list of memories of their experiences. What's important, however, is whether you want or need them to remember the experience well enough to follow directions, repeat it, recount it, or duplicate it. Much of education is about creating mental models for students to use and follow.

New cognitive models can often revolutionize an audience's understanding of data, information, or an experience by helping them understand and reorganize things they previously understood (or, perhaps, couldn't understand), in a way that illuminates the topic or experience.

To create meaningful cognitive models, consider the ways in which you want your audience to find meaning and what you want them to remember. In most cases, you will need to choose one form for the overall experience (like the sequence of a book, play, or music, or the layout of a party, theme park, or building). There are no *right* answers to this one form, but you would be wise to explore different forms before settling on one (see *Information* on page 42 and *Multiplicity* on page 72). Of course, this form won't work best for everybody, so when it's important—and possible—create other ways of moving through the experience that allows others to form a mental map in a way that better suits them. Also, be wary of mental models that constrain your experience or cause cognitive disonance (when the mental map formed doesn't conform well to the reality of the experience) for your participants (see *Metaphors* on page 102).

Cognitive Models

photographs: Laurie Blavin

Cognitive Models

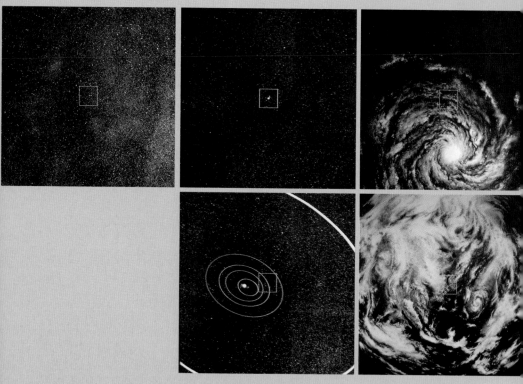

There have been few descriptions of our universe as powerful and astounding as the film *Powers of 10* made by Charles and Ray Eames and Phyllis and Phillip Morrison (now also a book). The size of the Universe and that of the atom are difficult for most people to grasp since these numbers are so vastly large and small (respectively); and, we have little way to relate them to what we can experience directly (the major way we create understandings).

This film takes us on a journey from 1 meter off the Earth's surface to the edges of the Universe—not in a direct or algebraic line (a journey that would be impossibly long) but an exponential one. In other words, instead of presenting pictures back toward the Earth at every meter thereafter, we see views that increase exponentially from one meter to 10 to 100 to 1000 etc., finally stopping at nearly one billion light years from the Earth.

Likewise, the second half of this journey takes us into increasingly smaller views (starting at the same point one meter above the surface of the Earth) until we move inside the body, its organs, cells, organelles, molecules, atoms, and finally to the edge of our understandings of the physical Universe: inside sub-atomic particles.

Powers of 10

isbn: 0716760088
www.eamesoffice.com/powers_of_ten/powers_of_ten.html

The film (and book) use this linear organization with constant intervals of distance to help us form a cognitive model of the relative sizes of the things we understand (and don't yet) in terms that we can begin to comprehend.

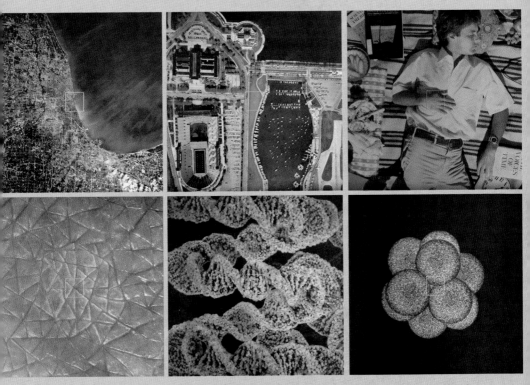

One of the most important, and unexpected, observations isn't how big or small things are, but that certain repeating patterns of vast emptiness and packed activity are almost constant from the sub-sub-sub atomic to the largest conceivable astronomical bodies. These kind of relationships draw conclusions about the nature of the Universe and even how we perceive, and these revelations also lead to a formation of a cognitive model for the Universe that anyone can understand.

creators: Phillip and Phyllis Morrison and Charles and Ray Eames
first published in 1968
photographs copyright Eames Office

Powers of 10

plumbdesign

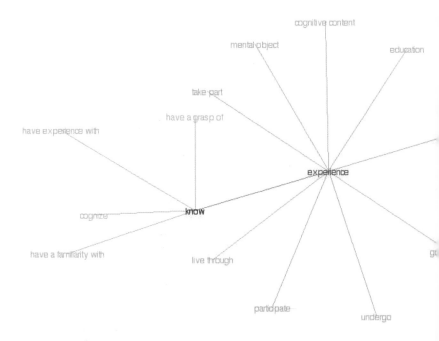

cognitive content

mental object

education

take part

have a grasp of

have experience with

experience

cognize   know

have a familiarity with

live through

go

participate

undergo

Sometimes the best cognitive models aren't aligned with known objects (as with metaphors) or environments (as with maps), but are abstract and reduce meaning to a more pure state. The Plumbdesign Thinkmap system is a diagramming system that relates terms, objects, or elements to each other in an abstract and cognitively reduced

Thinkmap Thesaurus

www.virtualthesaurus.com

experience design 1.1

umbdesign

cognitive content

content

have a break

live through
know

move

experience

have a travel experience with

go through

participate

take a step
take steps

take part

horizon

noun

verb

VISUAL THESAURUS

experience know participate experience

DISPLAY : ○ AUTO-NAVIGATE
○ 2D   ◉ 3D

adverb

CREATED USING TH!NKMAP

COPYRIGHT 1998 PLUMB DESIGN, INC

way. One of the effects of this is that there are no other meanings overlaid onto the cognitive space, and the cognitive model and presentation are aligned perfectly. Of course, this isn't necessarily the best solution for every use but, when it is, there are no more seductive presentations of these cognitive maps than the Thinkmap diagrams.

Thinkmap Thesaurus

experience design 1.1

One of the most difficult concepts for designers to understand is that

the presentation of an experience or design (its appearance) is separate from its organization.

Often, these are so tightly coupled or so commonly combined that we can't imagine a particular organization presented in any other way (geographic information, for example, presented as maps). However, the most common taxonomies for presenting information aren't always the most successful.

Almost any organization can be presented in a variety of ways. Textual data (words or numbers) can be presented in writing (such as a description), visually (as in any variety of charts), or aurally (as in live or recorded speaking), or in any combination.

Even map data can be presented in all of these ways. Consider driving directions to a house. The organization of the data most likely will be time and location (specifically, locations over time in an efficient route). However, these directions can be written into a descriptive paragraph, listed in a bulleted list, charted as a map in any of a variety of forms and projections, or recorded in sequence as an audio tape to played in real time.

This is often the case with political or legal presentations in which it is more important to the presentation's creators to incite a particular opinion than it is to be accurate or understandble. This is how propaganda and disinformation are formed. Unfortunately, it's often the outcome of visual design since most designers value visual style and appearance over understanding and accuracy (whether they realize it or not). While designers are *supposed* to bring something new and unique to the design process— often something unexpected or previously considered unrelated; sometimes these inspirational elements really aren't appropriate, or they are implemented in a way that obscures everything *but* the style.

Presentation

Presentation

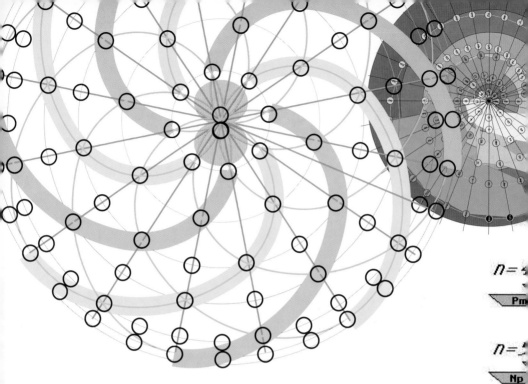

$n=4$

Pm

$n=3$

Np

$n=2$

While most of us are familiar with the now common diagram of the periodic table of elements, it is neither the oldest, nor the only form this information can take. In fact, there may be new forms for this information that can communicate new aspects of the relationship of atoms to one another and their importance to the forming of the world around us.

The periodic table that we have come to know has evolved over centuries as physicists have tried to make sense of the data they've observed about fundamental elements and atoms. The diagram has morphed in unexpected, novel ways (circles, figure-eight's, even three-dimensionally) in order to explain and reconcile the seemingly inconsistent data generated by increasingly sophisticated measurements. The largest of these diagrams presented here is my own, latest attempt to describe the relationship of elements in terms of the positions of their electrons and nuclei—literally the shape of the atoms themselves. (Although this is based on some still controversial opinions about the shape of atoms.)

It's always important to explore new ways of seeing and describing common phenomena as these explorations help us develop better understandings of what we have yet to know. All of these diagrams, in fact, are wrong—and always have been—though they have been the best explanations we've had to date.

Periodic Table of the Elements

You can explore the periodic table of the elements at www.chemicalelements.com.

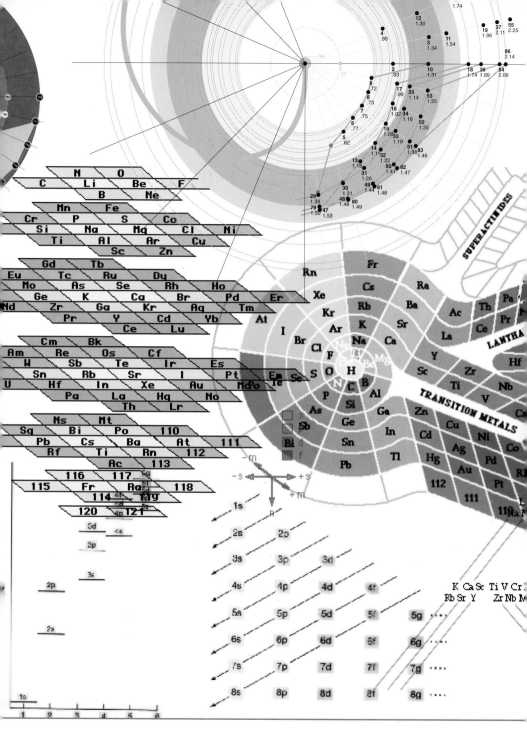

Models developed by Dr. Timmothy Stowe, Thoedor
Benfey, Emil Zmaczynski, and Nathan Shedroff

Periodic Table of the Elements

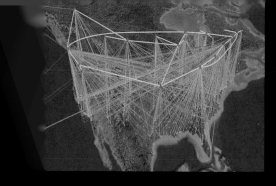

Artistic
    Geographic
        Cables & Satellites
        Traceroutes
        Census
        Topology
        Info Maps
            Info Landscapes
            Info Spaces
        ISP Maps
    Web Site Maps
    Surf Maps
    Muds & Virtual Worlds
Historical

An Atlas
Of Cyberspaces

Welcome to the Atlas of Cyberspaces

This is an atlas of maps and graphic representations of the geographies of the new electronic territories of the Internet, the World-Wide Web and other emerging Cyberspaces.

These maps of Cyberspaces — cybermaps — help us visualise and comprehend the new digital landscapes beyond our computer screen, in the wires of the global communications networks and vast online information resources. The cybermaps, like maps of the real-world, help us navigate the new information landscapes, being objects of aesthetic interest. They have been created by 'cyber-explorers' of many different disciplines from all corners of the world.

Some of the maps you will see in the Atlas of Cyberspaces will appear familiar, using the cartographic conventions of real-world maps, however, many of the maps are much more abstract representations of spaces, using new metrics and grids. The atlas comprises separate pages, covering different types of maps.

[Introduction | Conceptual | Artistic | Geographic | Cables & Satellites |
| Traceroutes | Census | Topology | Info Maps | Info Landscapes | Info Spaces |
| ISP Maps | Web Site Maps | Surf Maps | MUDs & Virtual Worlds | Historical]

Mapping Cyberspace
a new book by
Martin Dodge & Rob Kitchin
Published October 2000

Primary Atlas site
cybergeography.org

Mirror sites
North American
(provided by Peacock Maps)

European

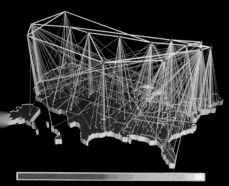

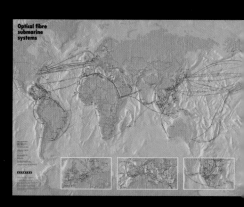

Optical fibre
submarine
systems

here are many ways to view the same thing, though we often become so accustomed certain, standard views that we take the possibilities for granted and forget to even plore alternatives.

s site contains a wealth of maps in a variety of forms that all describe, essentially, same thing: the size and activity of the Internet. This variety reminds us to search new—and better—ways to visualize and describe what we're trying to communicate.

as of Cyberspaces

w.cybergeography.org/atlas

book: *Mapping Cyberspace* by Martin
Dodge and Robert Kitchin
isbn: 0-415-19884-4
www.mappingcyberspace.com

perience design 1.1

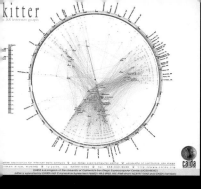

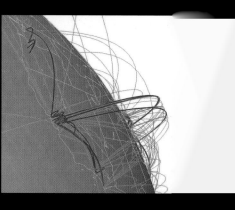

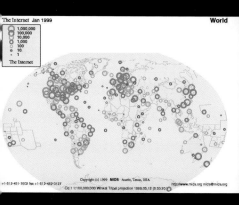

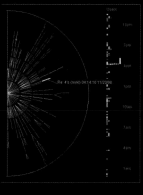

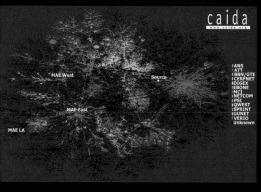

Atlas of

experien

Key to the development of cognitive models is the diversity of people's learning styles and abilities, as well as the complexity and depth of data in many circumstances. This is what creates the need for multiplicity in organizational schemes, both in redundant and alternative organizations as well as in deeper levels of organization that are layered onto higher-level organization to make an experience clear.

Multiple views and other redundancies may seem like a waste of time and resources, but the duplication is critical to creating understanding for a variety of people.

Since everyone has different skills and experience, no one way of organizing data is capable of creating understanding for everyone.

Varying organizations and presentations allow each person to best find his or her way. Examples of these multiple points of entry into content are book indexes and building signage. In search interfaces, they allow for multiple search criteria, including browsing, which itself is an alternative to searching.

Multiple organizations also support multiple points of views. In some interfaces, different paths that support different organizations clearly allow and shape different understandings in a body of content. This can create an opportunity   for richer understanding since conflicting perspectives often can lead to deeper thought and more consideration when forming not only opinions and understandings, but cognitive models as well.

Multiplicity

Most complex data require several levels of organization, varying the form of organization at each level to suit the content. Encyclopedia, guidebooks, and directories, for example, often nest their organizations. Directories might first list items by location, then by quality (or some other magnitude), and then alphabetically. These levels help break the data into meaningful chunks that can be navigated more easily. They also reflect and *create* hierarchies of importance and priorities, and thus, meaning.

Lastly, multiple levels of organization create a hierarchy for reading as well as importance. It's advisable, then, that the most important meaning (however this is deemed), also be the most evident (whether on a page or screen). In other words, importance should be reflected in obviousness, or at least, ease of reading. Likewise, the second level of

importance should be reflected in the next apparent data and organization, and so on. Unfortunately, many designs often use style to mask the hierarchy of importance thereby decoupling this relationship, making it more difficult to navigate as well as understand the meaning of the content itself.

Multiplicity

Most design works on many levels, often on levels that the viewer, participant, or user isn't even aware of throughout the experience. Some of these manifest themselves in emotional reactions that even unknowing bystanders don't understand. Maya Lin's Memorial to the Vietnam War in Washington D.C., ensures that no one becomes an innocent bystander—everyone is affected.

How this is done is subtly but wonderfully perfected. By combining simple forms of organization with an understated, yet haunting, presentation, she has personalized what is normally impersonal about war memorials.

The monument is a seemingly simple nexus of two black granite walls, inscribed with the names of the 58,183 US men and women who officially died during the Vietnam War. The fact that the names are there is unusual enough, but their organization is critical to the shape, form, and evocative nature of the memorial.

In essence, the wall is a statistical chart of deaths over time during the period from 1959 to 1975. Instead of a flat base (like a normal chart would have), the diagram is inverted, sloping into the earth, like a grave, and looming 10 feet high at its apex.

What gives the monument its structure is the organization of names (deaths) over time as the deaths gradually build from the early years, and then decrease as the US pulled

Vietnam War Memorial

www.virtualwall.org
Washington, D.C.

out of the region in the end. The actual graph has been simplified, of course, and the power traded for accuracy is more than worth the normalization of the graph.

Shortly after the monument was chosen as the winning design, the names were summarily reordered alphabetically because the jury felt that the chronological order would make it impossible for visitors to find loved ones—and they were correct. However, the power of the design—and the whole reason for its form—was suddenly diminished. In addition, the names themselves became less important as each of the 16 James Jones became indistinct. As originally conceived, the names of servicemen and women often would appear in relation to the others with whom they had died. Like any great work of art, the more one knows about the piece and its context (such as the names of soldiers from a battalion that suffered heavy loses at a particular battle), the more meaningful it becomes.

The answer was a multiplicity of organization that reordered the names as originally intended. Two podiums also were added at each side of the entrance to the monument that encased alphabetical directories of the names and locator panels. The addition not only restored the monument's original power and emotional potential, but the experience was made feasible in light of the needs of its visitors. The two organizations were essential in creating the necessary experiences.

designer: Maya Lin   **Vietnam War Memorial**

Everyone has a different need for the same things and a different way of finding them. In this case, it's furniture. What's nice about this site is that furniture is organized in multiple ways so that buyers can find what they want based on their needs or what they already know about the furniture. As is typical, furniture is organized by category (seating, storage, accessories, etc.), but there are also categorizations that organize and reference other attributes (gifts, eco-friendly items, furniture made from sustainable materials, and ways to browse furniture from a particular designer). The site lacks a good way of viewing everything they offer in a single view (think of a visual site map to a website), like that from the now defunct Herman Miller Red (the previous example this one replaces—see *Experience Design 1*). This means that customers lack important context in reviewing choices or understanding the full spectrum of possibilities or options. Nevertheless, it's easy to traverse pages and products and the site is certainly popular and successful.

Design Within Reach

www.dwr.com

GIFT SERVICES
Gifts
Gift Card
Gift Bag
Gift Tag

HIGHLIGHTS
Tools for Living
Custom Leather
Sonno Mattress Sale
New Products
Saarinen Pedestal Collection
Classics
On Sale

CATEGORIES
Seating
  New
  Sofas
  Sleep Sofas
  Chaise/Lounge
  Bar & Counter Stools
  Dining Chairs
  Task/Ergonomic Chairs
  Outdoor
  Stackable Chairs
  Chairs Under $200
  Benches & Ottomans
  Low Stools
  On Sale
  All Seating
Bedroom
Shelving/Storage
Tables
Lounge
Dining
Workspace
Lighting
Outdoor
Accessories
Floor Coverings

SOLUTIONS
Sleep Sofas
Media Storage
Stackable Chairs
Extendable Tables
Chairs Under $200
Eco-friendly
Small Spaces
Gift Card

VIEW ALL CATEGORIES

Seating

We're not online, but please leave a message

New

Sofas

Sleep Sofas

Chaise/Lounge

Bar & Counter Stools

Dining Chairs

Task/Ergonomic Chairs

Outdoor

Stackable Chairs

Chairs Under $200

Benches & Ottomans

Low Stools

Design Within Reach

There is no such thing as objectivity.

As much as we would like to believe otherwise and for all the repeating of this mantra in our educational system, it simply isn't true. Every part of the process of communicating is subject to the values, perspectives, and understandings of those creating the content.

This doesn't mean that we can't make a point of trying to be "objective," or more accurately, to present meaning with as little hyperbole and sensationalism as possible. Indeed, the best understandings are formed from presentations of differing, balanced views and opinions. What this means, however, is that even acts as simple and seemingly innocent as organizing data are subjective. Indeed, organizing data and the creation of information may have a profound impact on its meaning.

Even the documents that we think of as so basic that they are free of subjectivity, are actually rife with it. Dictionaries, for example, are organized simply (alphabetically), but the words themselves—as well as their meanings—are included through an often highly subjective process. This isn't necessarily bad. Subjectivity is necessary for the communication of opinion and personal stories. The problem arises only when we deny the existence of subjectivity at all levels (including the deepest and most "basic") of communication.

Subjectivity

Subjectivity

Most journalism seeks to ignore and even mask its own values and biases by decree of objectivity. This, of course, is a lie—but a common and generally accepted one. Instead of denouncing its role in the creation of opinion, COLORS makes this inevitability a cause to celebrate, and influence. Never denying its goals, it presents some of the most moving testimony to the complexity and wonder of cultures around the world.

COLORS Magazine

www.benneton.com

Creator: Tibor Kalman

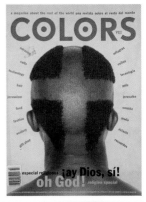

Through photography and text, both wonderfully reflecting its point-of-view and consciousness of the power of juxtaposition, COLORS has created one of the most refreshing views on the world. And, astonishingly, those views are, in some ways, more "objective" and more powerful than those produced by the mainstream media.

COLORS Magazine

The quality of any knowledge depends on the quality of perspective, and the character of the information. Salon is a site that presents top-notch writing without leaving out the perspective. In fact, it is precisely this perspective that makes these stories so valuable.

Salon Magazine

www.salon.com

There's usually more than one way to get anywhere.

The same should be true with many experiences, at least with informing experiences as opposed to entertaining ones. Entertainment experiences, like stories or other narratives, tend to be one-way only because the story is told from a particular and deliberate point of view.

If possible, you should offer your audience several ways to navigate the experience, and this tends to be fairly easy with digital media. Even non-digital experiences, like books, can be more navigable with a bit of innovative thinking. Concepts like "links" or "jump words" can work just as well in print. However, they're often more difficult to implement and much more difficult to maintain and update, as they can be for online content. There are several examples of innovative books that try to link information throughout the book by concept and relationship. Indexes and directories are other, established ways of navigating static media and work just as well in digital experiences. Likewise, tables of content are merely another form of navigation already common to print media and accepted by audiences.

Many websites have a "site map" that, supposedly, is a visual way of accessing the entire site on one page. Of course, these are usually difficult to maintain—especially for larger, dynamic sites—so these "maps" are nothing more than lists (in other words, indexes). To compound the problem, many Web developers only put high-level links in these maps so that the index is only slightly more useful than the horizontal navigation throughout the site. The trick to making a useful site map is to organize as much of the site's content in one place and present it as clearly as possible.

Other forms of navigation also can use any kind of map or chart as a navigable presentation of a data set, when appropriate. Sometimes, these can orient people more easily than simple lists.

Wayfinding is an important, though subtle, aide to navigation. Wayfinding elements, or passive navigation, help orient users to where they are and where they can go. Technically, wayfinding elements, like street signs, don't actually need to function. In other words, they aren't the links and buttons themselves. Instead, they are the labels on pages and sections, the symbols, icons, or other visual elements that help orient people—even the rollover highlights that signal which of several options have been chosen.

Navigation

Important to wayfinding is usually the persistence of all navigational choices at any level. Users usually find it easier to orient themselves if the navigational choices they haven't chosen don't disappear as they move through a site. This can be difficult if there are a lot of navigational choices (which may signal another problem anyway) since they will take space on the screen and can, potentially, add to the noise and clutter. However, it is common for sites to keep "horizontal" or categorical navigation persistent in the navigation on every page (usually at the top). These choices allow users to begin a new path in a new category if the one they have chosen happens to be unhelpful. The "vertical" or deep navigation can be represented in a number of ways–as long as it *is* represented. The reason for this is to allow people to backtrack easily without restarting from the beginning.

One convention for presenting vertical navigation is the **directory path**. This line of linked text is a representation of the steps between the homepage and wherever the user is at the moment, functioning as a kind of digital trail of breadcrumbs. This allows people to not only move between the pages represented in this path but simply to review the path to orient themselves if they find that they are lost.

Cascading menus are another convention that presents pop-up menu choices at each step in a navigational menu, allowing users to jump to any page in a site by rolling over the right combination of menu choices. These systems can be useful if the set of pages are applicable to a lot of people, but they can be confusing. If it's likely that users have use for only a few pages of a site (or certain sections), such a menu system is probably overkill.

Fish-eye views are another way to navigate data sets and websites. These views essentially show the entire set of data or pages but allow the user to focus on one section at a time. In this way, users get a sense of the whole data set (size and shape) but they aren't bombarded with so much data that they become confused. Users can then move the focus around the data set to explore and reveal what they're after. Inxight Software offers a tool for building and managing just this kind of view. These can be useful for large, disparate site maps, for example.

People often perform the role of navigational advisor. Some sites offer live customer service in which people can be consulted in real time, and pages can be pushed to users as needed to help them find that which they're interested. Several companies offer tools to manage these types of services. These **guides** don't have to be real people. Some can be computational processes of the system that form a kind of consultative interface. *Guides 3.0* from Apple Computer was an experimental interface using the personification of data markers and algorithms as characters. These characters are composites of data and have no real personality, yet they can embody a point of view more clearly for most users. However, characters are difficult to create well and shouldn't be implemented merely to make an interface "cool."

Navigation

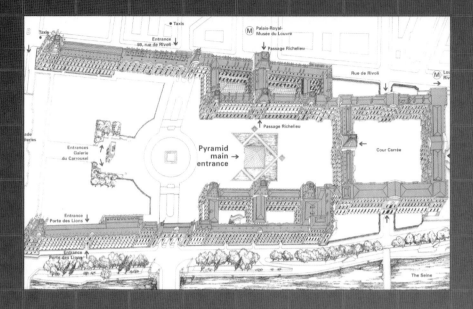

All signage systems are, essentially, about navigation and most are perfectly adequate—although too many are not. The Louvre's signage system is particularly successful, considering the complexity of the space it describes. The Louvre is an old building with irregularly shaped rooms and corridors. Most visitors find it daunting, if not for its overall shape then surely for its size.

The Louvre signage never abandons or abstracts the Louvre layout, rather it uses a grid system overlayed over the actual building, thereby regularizing the building without obscuring its detail. Then, each grid square can be referenced individually for location. Signage for each area quickly orients visitors to the three main wings of the museum. Highlights stand out in white against the gray background, the black building, and grid outlines.

This system isn't foolproof and I'm sure that people can still get lost or disoriented in the cavernous wings and rooms, but it does provide an outstanding way of orienting people in order to limit this problem.

Le Louvre

Le Louvre, Paris, France

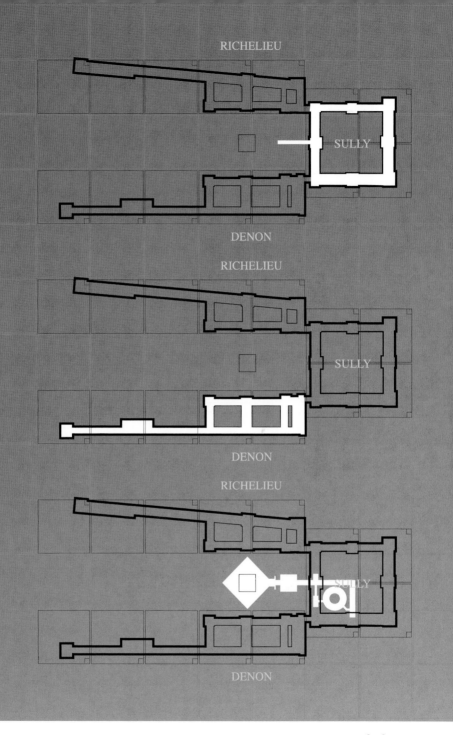

RICHELIEU

SULLY

DENON

RICHELIEU

SULLY

DENON

RICHELIEU

SULLY

DENON

Le Louvre

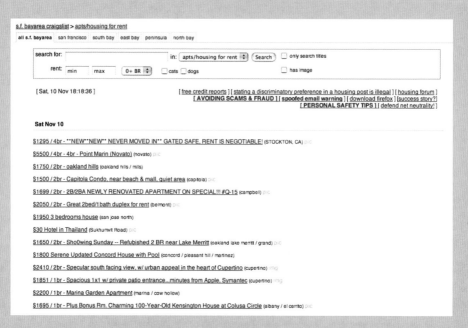

At first look, Craigslist may be overwhelming. The home page (and those of any other location) is filled completely with text links of some kind. Graphics on the site are nearly non-existent. Users must rely completely on the categorization and differences in typography to distinguish categories from sub-categories, links from headings, and determine where they need to go.

Nevertheless, the site is successful and works well. It's a great example of clarity being more important than simplicity. A simple site would only offer a few options (categories, perhaps). Each successive page would drill down a little more, uncovering a new level of sub-category until, pages later, people would eventually find what they seek. Instead, the homepage is filled with options, but easily distinguished ones. These don't just speed people to their destination, but they provide needed context about the boundaries and options available.

Craigslist is a breeze to navigate despite this complexity and each page, as is common nowadays, includes a record indicating the depth inside a particular category (and makes these links so users can easily backstep to any level in just one click). Filters allow people to narrow the results (whether filter or browsing) to smaller, more appropriate geographic areas.

Because the site is free (for all but a tiny number of categories (housing in NYC and jobs elsewhere), newspapers are finding it increasingly difficult to maintain their Classified Ads revenue. But, being free isn't the only differentiation here. Craigslist is easier to use and navigate than either the traditional newspaper classifieds section or their online counterparts, giving it an edge difficult for traditional approaches to surpass.

Craigslist

www.craigslist.org

craigslist

san francisco bay area W sfc sby eby pen nby

post to classifieds

my account

help, faq, abuse, legal

search craigslist

| | |
| for sale ▼ | > |

event calendar

S	M	T	W	T	F	S
4	5	6	7	8	9	10
11	12	13	14	15	16	17
18	19	20	21	22	23	24
25	26	27	28	29	30	1

avoid scams & fraud
craigslist factsheet
best-of-craigslist
job boards compared
weather quake tide
lawsuit dismissed
craigslist movie & dvd
craigslist T-shirts
craigslist foundation
progressive directory
defend net neutrality

system status

terms of use   privacy
about us   help

community

activities	lost+found
artists	musicians
childcare	local news
general	politics
groups	rideshare
pets	volunteers
events	classes

personals

strictly platonic
women seek women
women seeking men
men seeking women
men seeking men
misc romance
casual encounters
missed connections
rants and raves

discussion forums

1099	gifts	pets
apple	haiku	philos
arts	health	politic
atheist	help	psych
autos	history	queer
beauty	housing	recover
bikes	jobs	religion
celebs	jokes	rofo
comp	kink	science
crafts	l.t.r.	shop
diet	legal	spirit
divorce	linux	sports
dying	loc pol	t.v.
eco	m4m	tax
educ	money	testing
etiquet	motocy	transg
feedbk	music	travel
film	npo	vegan
fitness	open	w4w
fixit	outdoor	wed
food	over 50	wine
frugal	p.o.c.	women
gaming	parent	words
garden	pefo	writers

housing

apts / housing
rooms / shared
sublets / temporary
housing wanted
housing swap
vacation rentals
parking / storage
office / commercial
real estate for sale

for sale

barter	arts+crafts
bikes	auto parts
boats	baby+kids
books	cars+trucks
business	cds/dvd/vhs
computer	clothes+acc
free	collectibles
furniture	electronics
general	farm+garden
jewelry	games+toys
material	garage sale
rvs	household
sporting	motorcycles
tickets	music instr
tools	photo+video
	wanted

services

beauty	automotive
computer	household
creative	labor/move
erotic	skill'd trade
event	real estate
financial	sm biz ads
legal	therapeutic
lessons	travel/vac
	write/ed/tr8

jobs

accounting+finance
admin / office
arch / engineering
art / media / design
biotech / science
business / mgmt
customer service
education
food / bev / hosp
general labor
government
human resources
internet engineers
legal / paralegal
manufacturing
marketing / pr / ad
medical / health
nonprofit sector
real estate
retail / wholesale
sales / biz dev
salon / spa / fitness
security
skilled trade / craft
software / qa / dba
systems / network
technical support
transport
tv / film / video
web / info design
writing / editing
[ETC]   [part time]

gigs

computer	event
creative	labor
crew	writing
domestic	talent
	adult

resumes

usa		canada	countries
alabama		alberta	argentina
alaska		brit columbia	australia
arizona		manitoba	austria
arkansas		n brunswick	bangladesh
california		newf & lab	belgium
colorado		nova scotia	brazil
connecticut		ontario pei	canada
delaware		quebec	caribbean
dc		saskatchwn	chile
florida			china
georgia		**ca cities**	colombia
guam		montreal	costa rica
hawaii		toronto	czech repub
idaho		vancouver	denmark
illinois		more ..	egypt
indiana			finland
iowa		**us cities**	france
kansas		atlanta	germany
kentucky		austin	great britain
louisiana		boston	greece
maine		chicago	hungary
maryland		dallas	india
mass		denver	indonesia
michigan		houston	ireland
minnesota		las vegas	israel
mississippi		los angeles	italy
missouri		miami	japan
montana		minneapolis	korea
nebraska		new york	lebanon
nevada		orange co	malaysia
n hampshire		philadelphia	mexico
new jersey		phoenix	micronesia
new mexico		portland	netherlands
new york		raleigh	new zealand
n carolina		sacramento	norway
north dakota		san diego	pakistan
ohio		seattle	panama
oklahoma		sf bayarea	peru
oregon		wash dc	philippines
pennsylvania		more ..	poland
puerto rico			portugal
rhode island		**int'l cities**	russia
s carolina		amsterdam	singapore
south dakota		bangalore	south africa
tennessee		berlin	spain
texas		buenosaires	sweden
utah		dublin	switzerland
vermont		hongkong	taiwan
virginia		london	thailand
washington		manila	turkey
west virginia		mexico	UAE
wisconsin		paris	UK
wyoming		riodejaneiro	US
		rome	venezuela
		sydney	vietnam
		tokyo	

Craigslist

Visualization

Visualization of understanding is much more important than merely making something look "good." Visualization is integral to communication—as it *is* the organization made visible. Often, data and organization (and thus understanding) gets concealed when the type of visualization doesn't match the organization or the goals of the communication; or the visualization so highly distorts it that it is difficult to see.

Lists and diagrams come in a variety of types and forms and each has its best use. Timelines, maps, and charts (pie, bar, fever, and other types) are all types of diagrams that can illuminate—or obscure—meaning. Pie charts, for example, only work well when the number of data categories are few (no more than 10), and are varied in size (percentage); otherwise, bar charts are useful precisely when pie charts aren't. A good understanding of diagrams starts with exposure to the variety, as well as the realization that while almost any data can be presented in any style of diagram, like organizations, the results will vary in effectiveness.

Charts and maps are particularly useful for layering multiple data sets on top of each other to show relationships between the sets; in order to be effective, though, the scales and coordinates must be consistent and relative. This is especially true of three-dimensional (3D) diagrams as any problems of scale get more distorted (and inaccurate) with each dimension added. Generally, 3D diagrams and visualizations are used gratuitously and without an understanding or concern for the actual meaning of the data. Very few 3D charts actually illuminate data, but are used instead to fancify and "dress it up." This is *always* an inappropriate use of a technique.

Good visualizations pay special attention to **scale** (relative or absolute), **orientation**, **view**, **projection** (especially in the case of maps), **detail**, **generalization**, and **layers**. Some effective diagrams can use not only representations of three dimensions to represent three aspects of the data, but use color-coding and/or symbols to introduce from one to six more dimensions into the chart. The more dimensions, the more potential for clutter, but with careful consideration, some diagrams can be remarkably clear while displaying 8D data sets.

Visualization

NASDAQ Market Site

National Association of Security Dealers, Inc.
4 Times Square, New York City, NY 10036
www.nasdaq.com

experience design 1.1

Visualizing the data from the stock market has always been a concern of market traders, most of whom still prefer fast text-based interfaces and displays. The market wall at NASDAQ's Times Square lobby in New York City is an example of a visualization of the top-trading companies and market indicators displayed across a large wall that lets people quickly assess market conditions based on patterns and colors.

While this isn't a presentation that traders could probably use to watch specific stocks (as there's still a lot of noise), it's a successful overview for those who want overall impressions and market context. The color-coding of the companies is especially helpful as it allows for these quick impressions of overall conditions. Red is used to show declines, and the amount of red corresponds to the amount of decline. Likewise, green is used to show advances, and blue is the neutral color which is used to compare the ups and downs.

NASDAQ Market Site

date opened: December 1999

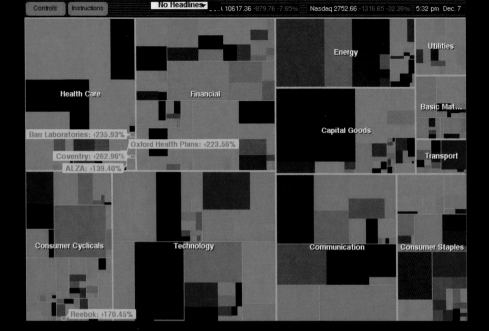

One of the most remarkable visualizations created in the last decade is the Map of the Market, a real-time map of the US stock market viewed as a graphical, colorful diagram where every part of the visualization has meaning and communicates information. What makes this most important isn't that it's new or even that it's innovative, but that it's *usable*. In fact, it's an incredible way to view a complex data set that is organized around the salient points of an investor's concerns.

Smart Money's Map of the Market

www.smartmoney.com/marketmap

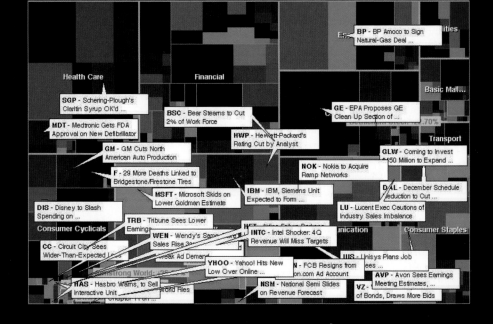

The map itself shows the entire market volume as a rectangle, which is marked-off into industries and companies by volume. The most important companies in a particular industry are grouped together and the size of their block is relative, in value, to their competitors. Each block is then color-coded based on its gain or loss at that moment. Lastly, company names and related headlines can appear when the cursor is placed on the blocks. There isn't much more to this map and that's important. (There doesn't need to be much more for it to be useful.) In fact, it is so stunningly clear, it's almost anticlimactic.

Smart Money's Map of the Market

Consistency uncovers a key dimension of experience: Breadth. All humans create a gestalt around the experiences we have through time. Where experiences relate, our expectations are that they will share consistent traits. Unfortunately, most constructed experiences—especially complex ones created by big organizations—fall short of this consistency because these experiences are devised, managed, and controlled via different people, departments, and even companies. Even though the identity may be consistent, the goals, messages, and triggers are often divergent—and confusingly so. Experiences that are consistent across the breadth of all customer touch-points feel more whole, understandable, and reliable than those that aren't.

Branding is built successfully, for example, when different experiences, often in different media, feel consistent and connected. Again, what is important is the cognitive level of consistency—that is, that the experiences *feel* similar and related, even if the details are quite different. Because media differ greatly in their strengths, weaknesses, and how people perceive them, transmedia design must deliberately mutate in order to take advantage of these differences and to be successful in each. What is carried away from the different media types is the feeling of connection that comes when the overall experience and some elements are consistent overall. The mistake that many designers make is in trying to design once for all circumstances. While this is always an ideal goal, this is rarely possible and usually results in experiences that aren't quite successful in any media, though very much consistent overall.

Consistency

Consistency is often **treated as** an end in itself—**especially with regards to the attributes within an experience, as opposed to between related experiences.** While it is always a good idea for elements of an experience—especially informational ones—to be consistent, sometimes it can actually get in the way of navigation or understanding. Because life is often inconsistent and, thus, people's experience is often inconsistent, consistency can sometimes be confusing when it is inconsistent with how we view and operate in the world. Therefore, a good measure of whether consistency works is to compare it with the expectations users have for the behavior of the experience or system. Because consistency is a cognitive process, it is something that must work for us mentally, and the only way to check this is to test the experience with real users in situations as close to real as possible.

This is not a license to create inconsistent experiences—unless confusion or disorientation is the goal or challenge of the experience (as with some games). Like metaphors (see page 102), it's important to ease-off on consistency if it is actually interfering with users' assumptions, and a strict adherence to consistency shouldn't prevent designers from doing this.

Consistency

Webby Awards

www.webbyawards.com
creator: Tiffany Shlain
date: held annually since 1996

experience design 1.1

Tiffany Shlain, the founder of the Webby Awards, and her small but creative team make it a point to break the conventions of most awards ceremonies. For example, they limit acceptance speeches to five words (significantly enhancing the responses and shortening the ceremony itself). They also try to maintain a sense of humor and context throughout the awards, and the pace is fast with lots of unexpected turns.

The Webby team knows that the experience doesn't just begin when people walk into the auditorium. There is a series of celebrations the night of the awards (pre and post awards), and the exterior of the auditorium building itself becomes a canvas to be transformed. 2000's awards featured an elaborate altar inside (for nominees to presumably pray at), which included a hidden camera so that curious quests seeking a closer view of the altar were unaware that their faces were being broadcast 40 feet high inside the auditorium until they, too, were face-to-face with the broadcast.

The Webbies also extends the experience before the ceremony in the form of elaborate, original invitations and announcements. At the awards, guests found a lunchbox with goodies inside, including an energy bar to help them make it through the ceremony.

Lastly, this multi-dimensional experience is extended onto the Web where the whole world can vote for its choice of best website in each category. Also, the ceremony and parties are webcast simultaneously (one of the most appropriate examples of a webcasted event).

Webby Awards

Apple is probably the most recognized innovation company in the world, at the moment. Not only is Apple constantly improving its product lines or introducing new products—often breakthroughs in the market—but it knows better than most companies the need to consistently offer experiences across all of is touchpoints.

It hasn't always been so, but much of Apple's success is due to this consistency. It used to be that consistency was a visual thing, ensuring that logos, colors, and other elements of corporate identity were used appropriately and similarly on everything the company made. However, consistency needs to extend into the experience as well.

Apple, and other companies, understand that it's not enough to produce wonderful products that customers want—and badly. They also must accompany these products with services that don't feel foreign to the company. Usually, when you call a company, whether its headquarters or customer service center, you don't feel like you're talking to the same company you bought your product from. The tone may be different, or the person's manners and personality—if you can talk to a person at all. Invariably, they may not have access to data in other parts of the company, may not know who you are, and may not be empowered to truly help you.

Apple, Inc.

www.apple.com

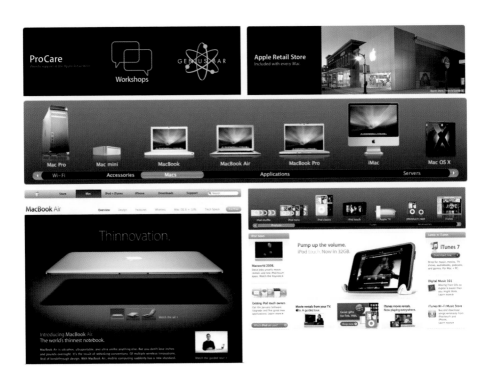

When you call Apple, however (whether you call Apple's store or customer service), you feel like you're talking to the same company who made the wonderful experience around the product you bought. This is no small feat. Apple's representatives (and that's truly what they are) are empowered to help, have access universally to the same data throughout the rest of the company (including your history with them), and uphold as much of the attributes that make up the Apple brand as possible.

Apple even opened its own stores because it had so little control over the retail experience—and it's paid off. With uncluttered interiors, clean surfaces, easy-to-find and try products, free WiFi and plenty of knowledgeable salespeople, Apple Stores are considered unthreatening, welcoming, and one of the best retail experiences to emulate. It goes deeper than store design and sales training, however. One of the ground-breaking innovations that consistently exudes the Apple brand, is the Genius Bar. This simple innovation ensures that customers can always find someone who can help them, no matter their problem or level of comfort with technology. In addition, Apple offers personal care and training, ProCare professional-level service, workshops, and even free design advice in stores with an Apple Studio. Throughout all of these experiences, and because of them, Apple's brand experience comes through reliably and clearly.

Apple, Inc.

Metaphors are one way to build a *cognitive model* (see page 60), and they can be very powerful in orienting people to help them understand an experience; but they can be equally disastrous if they aren't applied well. Metaphors use references to already known experiences as clues to new ones. The "desktop" metaphor of most personal computer operating systems is an attempt to help people create and use files, store and arrange them, delete them, and work with them. It has mostly worked well, but only because the metaphor isn't totally consistent with the real experience—the operating system doesn't *really* work like a person's desk. Too close of an adherence to the theme either limits the functions of the system, or creates confusion when the two don't work together consistently.

In actuality, most metaphors used in this sense are actually similes. The difference is subtle but was astutely pointed out by Brenda Laurel in her book *Computers as Theater*. It's worth noting in the context of experience design because it is possible to design experiences that are true metaphors. New devices and unique, playful theater or product experiences can actually redirect interaction with one object into manipulations of another. Before, a computer interface might visually represent the directory file system on its hard drive *as if* it were a desktop, in reality the two were not the same. However, researchers and designers are experimenting with objects that can behave metaphorically. Your imagination can open you up to the possibilities. A theme park like Disney's *Epcot Center* is a metaphor for the whole world, as Disney's new *California Experience* theme park is for the State.

Metaphors are not required and can be crutches for poor ideas and design. Used well, however, they can be illuminating for users and quickly orient them to the functions and interactions of an experience.

Metaphors

Computers as Theater, Brenda Laurel, Addison-Wesley, 1991, ISBN 081011313
new URLs: california Adventure, Epcot

photographs: Laurie Blavin

Metaphors

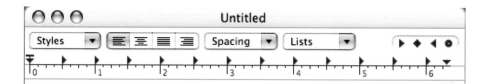

The Macintosh interface (known as the Desktop interface) isn't significant or successful because it was the first such interface (it wasn't), nor because it was the strictest, but because it was one of the first to recognize that any metaphor must be dropped when it becomes too cumbersome. Apple Computer got the idea for using the concept of a desk to organize documents and files on its new personal computer from the Xerox Star interface—well before the Star (barely) made it to market and promptly died a quiet death. Unlike most interface designs that copied the same idea, Apple spent a great deal of time extending, enhancing, and improving the idea.

One of the things that makes Apple's desktop metaphor successful is that it uses the metaphor judiciously to orient users to basic and important functions. The metaphor is dropped when it becomes difficult or impossible to reconcile the functions of the computer with the features of a real desk and papers. This gives it the flexibility to be reminiscent of the desktop without limiting the computer to only what a real desktop can do. (We don't usually put folders into other folders in the physical world, nor are we able to create magical folders of papers that are in two places at once.)

This metaphor has been extended considerably over the last 26 years and it's far from perfect, but it endures because the basic metaphor still orients users without limiting them.

Apple Macintosh OS X Desktop

www.apple.com/macosx

Apple Macintosh OS X Desktop

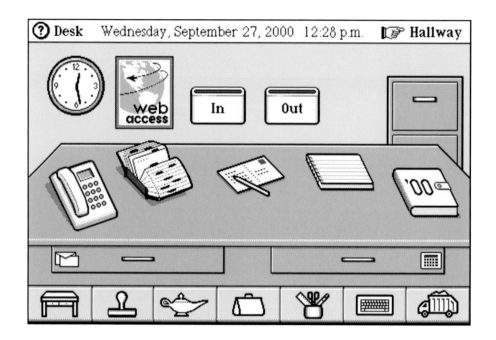

One of the first mobile devices with a unique interface, MagicCap was developed by General Magic in 1994 as one of the first PDAs (Persona Digital Assistants). In order to help familiarize users to such new and powerful features, the development team created a metaphor to contain most of its functions. This "room metaphor" organized all of the device's features into distinct rooms, which users could move between. The start room, which the device defaulted to upon turning on, contained a large desk representing common work applications as iconic objects, such as a calendar, clock, phone, drawers, etc

Outside of this room was a hallway which led to more rooms, such as a store room, game room, library, etc. Outside of the hallway was yet another metaphorical organizing level, called "Downtown." This was a "street" with buildings that represented different services, such as Internet connections, news, etc. In order to reduce the need to move between rooms, down the hallway or street, and other buildings, objects could be copied into places that automatically launched the services users expected in other places. While this cut down a bit on the need to "walk" down the street or hallway, it could never wholly replace the need to leave the main room (or desk).

MagicCap   Images form the MagicCap users manual.

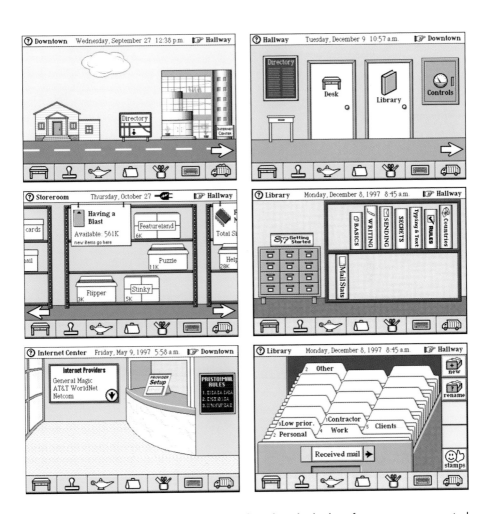

In order to hold true to the metaphor, most functions in the interface were represented metaphorically as common objects and rendered digitally to resemble these. Addresses looked like an address book, file folders had tabs, notebooks and spiral bindings, book corners could be folded over, etc. Like most metaphors, this helped users quickly become acquainted with the system but ultimately became tedious for experienced users.

MagicCap was expertly designed and executed but never saw wide release. As with metaphors in many other interfaces, the literalness of the metaphor was often extended further than it should, hampering usefulness (and often usability) in order to preserve consistency. When virtual objects in the interface stop behaving like their physical or literal counterparts, it's time to drop the metaphor in favor of more native behaviors.

MagicCap

Interface Design

Interface design is only one of many terms used for the design of experiences. It's a term that originated in the 1970s specifically for software interface design. Over the years it has expanded a bit to include not only software applications, but kiosk and CD-ROM interfaces as well. To some extent, website interfaces have been embraced by the general interface community; however, interface designers have resisted the expansion of the term to include print-based interfaces and other non-digital experiences, even though most of the approaches serve experience design in a greater sense.

You can think of interface design as encompassing information design, interaction design, and some forms of sensorial design (mostly visual and auditory design, since most computers can only display sights and sounds). Typically, interface designers have addressed the layout of screens, the design of screen elements like icons, and the flow among them.

There is a wealth of design knowledge and innovation within the interface design community, and most of it is not published on the Web. Many of the online industry's so-called innovations were already pioneered and developed within the interface community, and usually researched more thoroughly than the solutions created recently.

Mostly, interface design is concerned with the effectiveness and usability of a software interface but this should also extend to the usefulness and purpose of the product too.

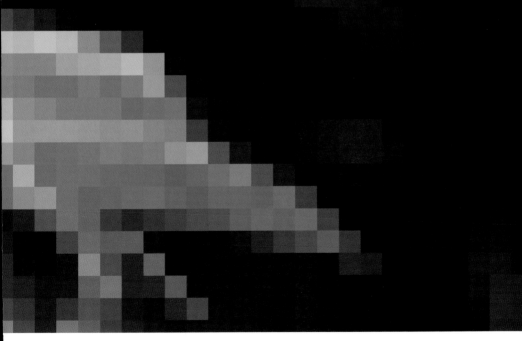

Interface Design

Usability is one of the battle cries of the traditional interface designer, as well as for those designing websites—usability applies to all experiences on some level. Unfortunately, it has become somewhat hackneyed, though nonetheless important; and, in some cases, its proponents have misstated and misused the concerns, processes, and results of usability to such an extent that its reputation has been tarnished. For sure, the concern for a product or experience's ease of use often takes a back seat to the concerns of schedules, budgets, and even appearance. However, usability is sometimes also used to squash innovation or to enforce the status quo.

To be effective, usability principles should always be verified with **user testing**. This means that design solutions should be tested in a neutral manner with users as close to the target maket as possible, who have not been exposed to the design-process solution. Those conducting the user testing also need to be careful not to lead their users through the test (and therefore subtly help them), to interpret the results objectively, and to base the redesign on the results of the testing.

Usability encompasses many factors. **Learnability** (the ease with which people can understand the experience/interface/product/service and begin using it), and **functionality** (how easy it is to use the experience once it is learned) are the two basic elements. These are often two very different and mutually exclusive phenomena. Designers may have to set their goals on one or the other rather than expect to achieve both. The reason for this is that the cues necessary to help a novice easily learn what to do are usually exactly the things that get in the way of experienced participants in using the system quickly, easily, and efficiently. Sometimes, two different interfaces to the experience (one for each group) might be better than one.

One of the things that most impacts functionality is **memorability** (how easy is it to remember what to do and when to do it). Experiences that are memorable tend to be easier to repeat successfully—especially since people may *want* to repeat them more as a result. Memorability is directly affected by the cognitive model (see page 60) people build in their minds about the experience. Clearer, more natural cognitive models (or those standard with our expectations) are built more successfully and are easier to remember. These tend to reduce errors as well as raise confidence and satisfaction for users. Easy **error recovery** is another consideration that, while not making the experience necessarily easier to learn or use, does increase satisfaction and decrease fear and frustration when errors do occur. Easily recovered errors are those that don't end the experience, or require it to restart from some prior point, or require previously finished work to be redone.

Usability (or a concern for "ease of use") is often the starting point of innovative design. When we approach preconceived solutions with fresh eyes—often those of our audience instead of our own—we're better able to create more satisfying experiences. Sometimes the roadblock to people being successful in an experience isn't that they don't understand how to use the experience but that they don't understand what to expect from it or why it might be valuable to them—concerns that designers almost never consider since they can't imagine their audience not understanding what they are trying to accomplish.

Usability

Usability

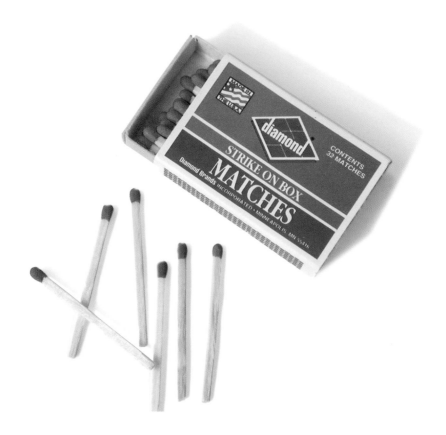

Matches are about as simple and as clear a device as you will find. Of course, they are only half the solution, requiring a suitable surface to strike them against. However, a match's operation has been reduced to a minimum of steps and a minimum of possible mistakes.

A Match

A Match

One of the most frustrating things in our lives is dealing with the difficulty in reconciling your desire to help and improve things with practicality of acomplishing something for a greater good. We aren't always sure if something will really improve a situation, if the money will be well spent, if the organization is credible, or if the people in need will really benefit.

The Hunger Site makes this effortlessly easy—so easy, in fact, it's a no-brainer. All you do is simply click a button, and a meal (or one of many other benefits like free mammograms or purchasing an acre in a rain forest) is sent to someone who needs it. Each click is small, but when combined, they can have a tremendous effect.

This only works because the site creators, owners, and sponsors have done all of the work, including establishing their credibility. The site's usefulness and its usability have made it as simple and as clear as possible to help one another.

The Hunger Site

www.thehungersite.com

the breast cancer site

Register & Give
Shop & Help
Be A Sponsor
More You Can Do
Donation Totals
Common Questions
About Us
About Breast Cancer
Home

43,300 mothers, sisters and friends will die from breast cancer this year.

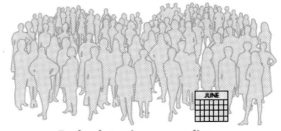

Early detection saves lives.

Donate Free Mammograms

the rainforest site

Register & Give
Shop & Help
Be A Sponsor
More You Can Do
Donation Totals
Common Questions
About Us
About Rainforests
Home

Almost two acres of tropical rainforest disappear every second.

2005

Donate Land - Free

The Hunger Site

Users interact with experiences in different ways, and this interaction can be a source of information for customizing the experience so that it responds differently for each user.

Experiences should, ultimately, change and modify themselves to be more appropriate for users.

It's conceivable, though undoubtedly difficult, for an experience to know a lot about its audience. For example, with computer-based experiences, computers can tell a lot about users, such as whether someone is present, how fast they are moving through the experience, whether or not they are running several programs, and whether they are splitting their attention among several programs. With real-time experiences, people controlling the experience can usually see how many people are present, if they're engaged sufficiently, how they're interacting, and whether or not they're understanding the experience, and so forth. Storytellers, for example, have been responding to user behavior and modifying their stories in real time for as long as stories have been told. It's the behavior of their audiences that allows them to adjust their stories to get the effects they're seeking.

There's no reason why an experience can't be designed to change based on how people react to it, whether the experience is digital, theatrical, or occurs in real space. Even small changes to only a few characteristics can make an experience feel more interactive (see *Adaptivity*, page184).

User Behavior

User Behavior

The best restaurants (those with outstanding cuisine and outstanding service) try to adapt as much as possible to their customers' needs, desires, and cultures. For example, the staff at Emeril's Delmonico in New Orleans is known to adjust their behavior to the culture of the diners at any given table.

Perhaps an older traditional couple at one table might be celebrating their anniversary and, as a result, expect to be distracted as little as possible and treated with the utmost respect that their age and experience suggest. Another table might be filled with younger diners who have no need, in fact a dislike, for pretense or tradition and prefer a waiter that smiles, laughs, and intrudes in a friendly way, possibly offering suggestions, making jokes, or engaging in personal conversation. These tables might be served by the same person, who adjusts and adapts his behavior based on whatever cues he can read from his customers (such as dress, demeanor, body language, conversation, tone, etc.).

Emeril's Delmonico

1300 St. Charles Ave, New Orleans, LA 70130
TEL 504 525 4937
The Venetian, Las Vegas Blvd. S., Las Vegas, NV 89109
TEL 702 414 3737
www.emerils.com/restaurants/delmonico

Not only does the chef willingly make substitutions on-the-spot to compensate for diners' food allergies, preferences, or customs (seeing it almost as a professional challenge), the restaurant even has been known to reconfigure a room during the course of a meal to position a group under the stunning chandelier in the Crystal Room when all of the other patrons have left. This commitment to adaptively building experiences creates moments of surprise and comfort and makes each diner feel special.

All experiences should strive to adapt themselves to the differences each customer or participant engenders.

creator: Emeril Lagasse
opened in 1997

Emeril's Delmonico

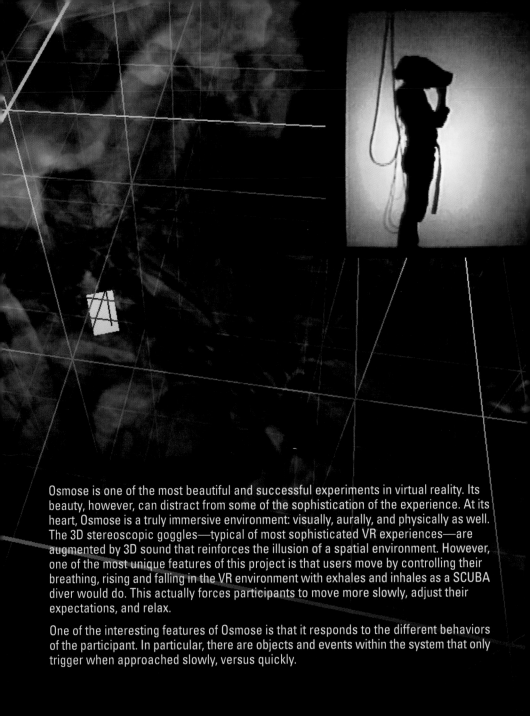

Osmose is one of the most beautiful and successful experiments in virtual reality. Its beauty, however, can distract from some of the sophistication of the experience. At its heart, Osmose is a truly immersive environment: visually, aurally, and physically as well. The 3D stereoscopic goggles—typical of most sophisticated VR experiences—are augmented by 3D sound that reinforces the illusion of a spatial environment. However, one of the most unique features of this project is that users move by controlling their breathing, rising and falling in the VR environment with exhales and inhales as a SCUBA diver would do. This actually forces participants to move more slowly, adjust their expectations, and relax.

One of the interesting features of Osmose is that it responds to the different behaviors of the participant. In particular, there are objects and events within the system that only trigger when approached slowly, versus quickly.

Osmose

www.immersence.com/osmose

principal designer: Char Davies
programmers and engineers:
Georges Mauro, John Harrison,
Rick Bidlack, and Dorota Blaszczak

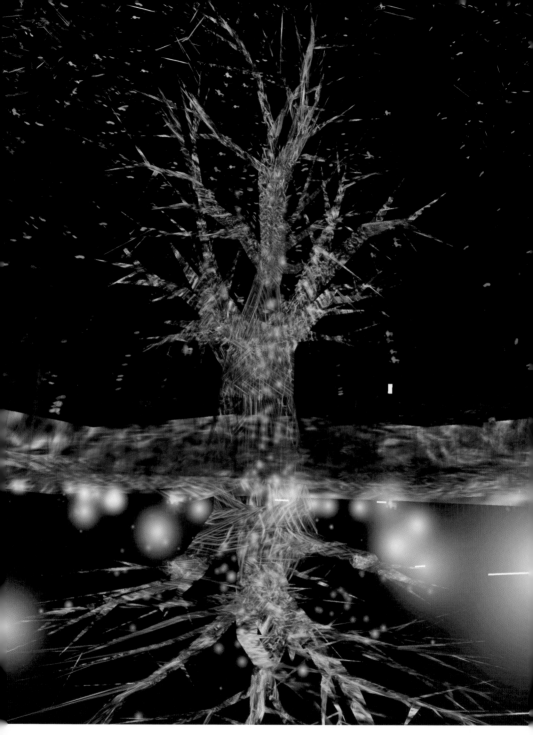

images copyright 2000 Immersence

Osmose

People express meaning through experiences and things based on a wide variety of personal values. Yet, meaning itself is universal. All people share similar core meanings, even if they express and prioritize them differently.

That people find meaning in things is, perhaps, the only constant that can be relied upon.

To this end, it's important to design experiences so that audiences or participants can connect meaning in them by making connections to their own lives and values—that is, if we want these experiences to have lasting impact. Meaning is *the most important* aspect of any experience—and often the most valuable one.

Meaning is the deepest level at which we can connect with others and transcends the other four levels of significance: performance, price, emotion, identity, and meaning.

Function: The most basic question someone can ask when evaluating a product, service, experience—or even ideology—is "Does this do what I need it to?" Companies, especially those in technology industries, *love* to focus on issues of performance and functional benefits, but too often, the products with the most or best features aren't the most successful.

Price: People often express concerns over price or value. Companies, too, focus on price and, less so, on providing value from their customers' perspective. Answering the question "Is this worth it?" is something both customers and organizations have learned to do well. But, it often doesn't allow companies to differentiate their offerings on anything other than price, which is a loose connection to customers and not one that loyalty or brands are built upon.

Emotions: many managers eschew these issues but the evidence that people buy largely along emotional lines is legend in the advertising world where this has been acknowledged at least since the 1960s. Emotions help customers answer the question "Does this make me feel good?" Of course, it's not always about "good." Sometimes, it is "scared," "excited," or "relaxed." All purchases occur within an emotional context and this is often so powerful, that customers make purchases that don't satisfy their needs of function and price as a result.

Status /Identity: Connecting to people's identities is all about answering the question "Is this me?" It is not as if products and services create our identity but we gather things around us that fit with the identities we've created for ourselves. This also represents an increasingly personal connection that becomes more individual and idiosyncratic as we move through these levels. This isn't good news for either designers or marketers as it represents increasing difficulty in understanding and delivering value at this deeper levels. This translates into higher expenses in research, development, localizing, distribution, and supporting offerings.

Meaning: This is the zenith of significance, the deepest point at which we can connect with our customers, and here, an interesting thing happens. While concerns and differences get increasingly difficult along this spectrum of significance, they actually reverse at this point, becoming universal and making it easier to design for many customers. At this level, the concerns of significance turn from the personal to the worldly—specifically, our sense of reality. The question people ask (almost entirely unconsciously) is "Does this fit my concept of the world?" In other words, people tend to more easily buy products, services, and experiences that fit how they understand the world, from the physical ("Is solar energy ready for primetime?") to the spiritual ("Is this what God expects of me?").

Meaning

Meaning is often evoked by objects and experiences that trigger core meanings that relate to our lives—that are the building blocks of values and emotions. Meaning is how we perceive and understand the world around us. Not every experience should, necessarily, have this as a goal but, often, the distinction of a successful or memorable experience is that it transforms us or makes us feel something that aligns with our deepest understandings of the world. Just like experiences that align with our identities—our sense of selves—meaningful experiences complement the world we live in (or, our view of it). **Artifacts** of an experience (physical objects from the experience) that remind us of that experience become valuable to us because they serve to remind us and help us relive those experiences. Therefore, artifacts of meaningful experiences become, themselves, meaningful artifacts. This is true of products, services, and events—whether virtual or physical.

The 15 core meanings so far identified include:

1. **Accomplishment**—achieving goals and making something of oneself; a sense of satisfaction that can result from productivity, focus, talent, or status. Examples: American Express' "membership has its privileges" and Nike's "Just Do It".
2. **Beauty**—the appreciation of qualities that give pleasure to the senses or spirit. Of course beauty is in the eye of the beholder and thus highly subjective, but our desire for it is ubiquitous. Beauty can be more than mere appearance. For some, it is a sense that something is created with an elegance of purpose and use. Examples include Bang & Olufsen and Jaguar.
3. **Creation**—the sense of having produced something new and original, and, in doing so, to have made a lasting contribution. Designers' lives and careers are all about acknowledging and participating at this level of meaning.
4. **Community**—A sense of unity with others around us and a connection with other human beings. Examples include any religious community, fraternities, or club.
5. **Duty**—the willing application of oneself to a responsibility. The military in any country counts on the power of this meaning, as do many employers. Duty can also relate to responsibilities to oneself or family. Commercially, anything regarded as "good for you," including vitamins, medications, and cushioned insoles, relays some sense of duty and the satisfaction it brings.
6. **Enlightenment**—clear understanding through logic or inspiration. This experience is not limited to those who meditate and fast, it is a core expectation of offerings from Fox News, which promises "fair and balanced" reporting, to the Sierra Club, which provides perspective on environmental threats and conservation.
7. **Freedom**—the sense of living without unwanted constraints. This experience often plays tug-of-war with the desire for security; more of one tends to decrease the other.
8. **Harmony**—the balanced and pleasing relationship of parts to a whole, whether in nature, society, ourselves, or in our homes.
9. **Justice**—the assurance of equitable and unbiased treatment.
10. **Oneness**—A sense of unity with everything around us. It is what some seek from the practice of spirituality and what others expect from good tequila.
11. **Redemption**—Atonement or deliverance from past failure or decline. Though this might seem to stem from negative experiences, the impact of the redemptive experience is highly positive. Like community and enlightenment, redemption has a basis in religion, but it also attracts customers to Weight Watchers, Bliss spas, and the grocery store candy aisle.
12. **Security**—the freedom from worry about loss. This experience created the insurance business, and it continues to sell a wide range of products from automatic rifles to Depends undergarments.
13. **Truth**—A commitment to honesty and integrity. This experience plays an important role in most personal relationships, but it also is a key component of companies like Whole Foods, Volkswagen, and Newman's Own, all of which portray themselves as simple, upright, and candid.
14. **Validation**—the recognition of oneself as a valued individual worthy of respect. Every externally branded piece of clothing counts on the attraction of this meaningful experience whether it is Ralph Lauren Polo or members Only, as does Mercedes Benz and the Four Seasons.
15. **Wonder**—Awe in the presence of a creation beyond one's understanding. While this might sound mystical and unattainable, Disney has been a master of this experience for decades, and this is what keeps the Concorde flying all of those years (none of which were profitable).

Meaning

While waiting in the departure lounge to board the Concorde on one of its final flights, my attention was diverted by an audible gasp from an elderly woman sitting near me. I looked to her and then followed her eyes out the window as the plane was towed to the gate. Her reaction was honest and reflexive. I knew by looking into her eyes (her hand was over her mouth) that she had looked forward to this for years—that she didn't think it would ever actually happen. She had spoken for more than half the people in the lounge who were all peering silently out the floor-to-ceiling windows as this graceful plane was towed into place.

The plane was cramped and small, the leather seats nice but no bigger than standard economy seats. The 30 year old entertainment system carried exactly 7 channels of music—hardly advanced by 2003 standards. But, none of this mattered. As old as these planes were and as unimpressive the interior accessories were, it was still a powerful and exciting symbol of the future—even if it was a future past.

The flight itself was fairly ordinary. There isn't much sensation of flying at Mach 2 and if it weren't for the yellow LCD display ticking past two times the speed of sound you wouldn't have noticed the speed. The service, of course, was wonderful, as were the food and drinks, but the view out the tiny windows was hazy so I couldn't even make out the curvature of the Earth.

The reason why the Concorde flew for so many years despite never really paying for itself was more than the prestige British Airways and Air France garnered for exclusively offering supersonic travel. The Concorde was a symbol of progress and the future as much as one of exclusivity and opulence. For sure, it had different meanings for different people but when Concorde service ended, it wasn't like other planes leaving service. Instead, there was a noticeable anxiety. While First Class service had long passed the Concorde in luxury on most every carrier, there was no replacement for the rest of what this plane represented. The Concorde evoked a sense of Wonder and Beauty about human accomplishment that no other passenger plane has matched.

Concorde

Concorde

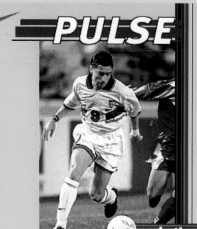

PULSE

" *I think, for me, it's been taking the ball one-on-one. Being able to* dominate one-on-one *situations. That's what's given me an* **advantage** *where other players have other types of advantages.* "

— TAB RAMOS

what's good about your game?

I'm fast on or off the pitch, and I almost always win the ball when someone tries to dribble over me.
Danny C.
age 16, Petaling Jaya, Malaysia

The best feeling in the world is to catch the ball while you are in the flight. I love that feeling.
Andrej M.
age 18, Murska Sobota, Slovenia

I am a good defender and I have mental and physical toughness so I can intimidate my opposition.
Clay J.
age 12, Lexington, Kentucky

I'm aggressive and I get back on defense quickly, which is very important.
Michael W.
age 13, Los Angeles, California

In 1997, while working on the first online strategy for nike.com, we helped Nike launch a series of online conversations with their customers in order to recast the Nike brand in terms that were approachable, personal, and meaningful. In order to create experiences around "little Nike" instead of "big Nike." The website, as well as several special event sites, were designed to allow customers to tell a bit of their own stories. Instead of being big and brash, representing the bravado typical of Nike's advertising, the website felt closer to a community (which it wasn't) with special stories no one else could get and ways in which the audience (mostly teenagers into sports) could contribute.

One of these experiences allowed the audience to answer a question about sports in their lives. Only a few answers would be published but they would appear alongside celebrity athletes, imparting a kind of equality of interest and importance that wasn't evident elsewhere. Even though the likelihood was so low of their answers being seen, thousands of people told the company about their lives and concerns. Likewise, when Tiger Woods was playing poorly in the US Open over Father's Day, his Nike fans sent words of encouragement and talked about the role their fathers played in their own lives and sports.

This site was able to engage its audience on the level of meaning with core meanings of Community, Accomplishment, and Validation in a way that few sites do today.

nike.com

vivid team: Lisa Bertelsen, Kevin John Black, Max Carmichael, Travis Curl, Ken Fromm, Nat Johnson, Dan Jones, Doris Mitch, Christian Mogenson, Sean Moody, Clancy Nolan, Derek Powazek, Stuart Rogers, Nathan Shedroff, Maurice Tani

KEEPING UP WITH TIGER

I was never into golf until Tiger Woods came along. Now, it's totally cool. One golfer said Tiger is Michael Jordan in long pants. I just say, Tiger is The Man!

Don't be nervous. Try to make the best shots you can and try to get in front.
Jimmy G, 8
Tigard, Oregon

Never give up because anything can happen, and don't get overconfident.
Randy R, 14
San Leandro, California

nike.com

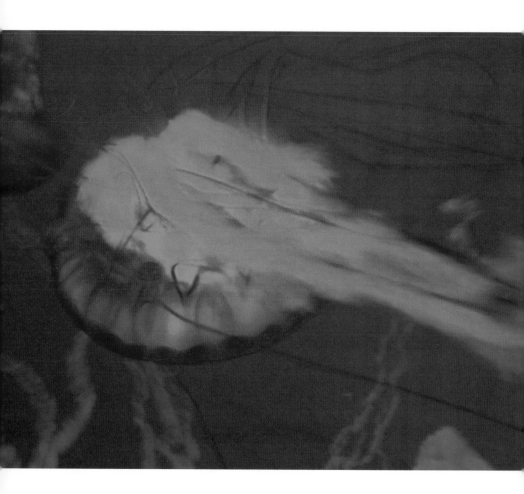

Like user behavior, experiences can be modified through an awareness of their users and their environments. In particular, experiences that modify themselves based on behavior seem more sophisticated. These changes might be environmental (temperature, humidity, ambient sounds, light, time of day, and so forth), technological (bandwidth, compatibility, or performance), as well as social (number of participants, types of relationships, subject matter, interaction with others, among other factors).

Awareness isn't necessary for experiences to be successful but it can be a vital component of sophisticated and more personal experiences.

Awareness

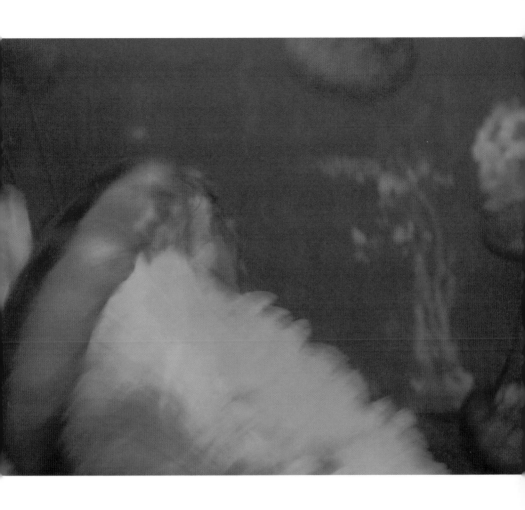

Awareness

There are few consumer products that we revere simply because of their behavior. Mostly we value products because of their features, either the number of features or their specific capabilities. Most consumer products, though lively, don't ever feel alive or animate, which is mostly due to the lack of awareness they have of their environments and the people around them. Even computers, which are endlessly flexible, capable, and configurable, haven't been programmed to be aware terribly of their surroundings or of the people who use them regularly.

Some exceptions to this condition are some simple home media products from Bang & Olufsen, a company renowned for its stunningly beautiful products as well as their relatively clear and easy operation—and now, their responsiveness to their owners.

Bang & Olufsen   multiple locations worldwide

www.bang-olufsen.com

One example is a B&O stereo that opens itself when a hand is poised in front of it (reacting to the presence of someone with the intent to play a tape or CD). Another is a television that turns itself toward the direction from which the remote control signal is coming, in order to position the screen toward the viewer no matter where he or she is sitting in a room. Another is a volume control that continuously monitors the ambient sound in a room and adjusts the volume of the stereo or television to remain consistently audible.

Any object can be built to be aware of its surroundings and the behavior of its users, but few have been. Indeed, computers and other products (like our homes themselves) know a great deal about us, but have made little or no use of this information so far.

Bang & Olufsen

Hello, Na

Buy now with 1-Click®
(you can always cancel it later)

Although it is extremely simply, the goodwill generated, as well as orientation and personal feedback, by the simple "Hello, ..." message at the top of Amazon's site is one of the reasons the experience of shopping at this online retailer is so satisfying to its customers. These messages are nothing new. However, Amazon was one of the first to make use of them (combined with its other customer service features such as 1-Click® ordering, suggestions based on past purchases, and reader reviews), and nowhere are these features put to better use than on this site.

These features have a direct correspondence to the physical world of shopping. Decades ago, when customers tended to shop repeatedly at the same local stores, store owners recognized these customers and treated them more like trusted friends. A welcome when they entered, and a recognition that they had visited before was only "common courtesy," and went a long way in establishing and maintaining a relationship.

While Amazon's offerings have ballooned, they have managed to present a plethora of choices (not just of products, but also of features) in a reasonably clear and accessible way.

Their awareness and acknowledgement of their customers allows them to build a more satisfying experience and a more trusted relationship. This isn't just due to the greetings but because the site reconfigures itself, to some extent, for each customer. It's *their* settings, recommendations, and past purchases that are displayed as their "usuals."

amazon.com

www.amazon.com

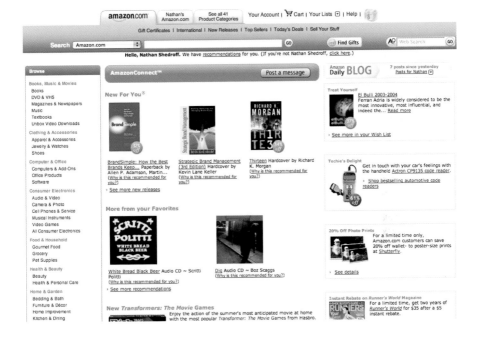

Interaction design is a discipline that specifically focuses on the interactivity between an experience and its audience. It's not that interaction designers ignore information design, visual design, or other principles, it is that they specifically focus on the invisible space between people and between people and things that form the experience with complex interactions that tax users. Interaction design is still relatively new and undocumented but growing as more interaction designers tackle and document their success and failures.

Overall experiences are usually more all encompassing than we first recognized. For example, consider the experience of shopping. To understand it from the perspective technologists usually take, shopping is merely the act of comparing product specifications until we're ready to make a purchase. But shopping as we know it in the real world is a complex, much more rewarding experience. In fact, the act of shopping usually begins before we even realize it—often before we perceive the need for something—and doesn't end until we finally discard and/or replace the product. Interaction designers are concerned with this distinction and are interested in exploring the complexity of real experiences in order to create new interactions that compare in richness and complexity, not merely in features.

Interaction design must take into account the totality of the experience in order to make to successful for people.

Interaction Design

Interaction Design

Technology is so seductive that those who work with it too often forget that the purpose of technology is to serve people's interests and needs. Ultimately,

what's important is not the technology but the people served by it.

Technological problems, in fact, are usually easy to solve (although economic viability is often the limiting factor). Meeting people's needs, however, is much more difficult—whether solved with technology or not. In fact, technology has become so sufficiently sophisticated that the limiting factors are less and less technical, and are now more social, cultural, and often political.

Technology should not be ignored—whether the technology in question is high-tech and computer-related or more traditional. Indeed, technology both enables and limits the experience that can be implemented, often creating an aesthetic of its own, the way art media are influenced by their technologies (compare, for example, tempera, oil, and watercolor paints). Rather, technologies need to be understood and implemented *after* the overall experience is designed, lest technologies drive the expereince toward unsatisfying outcomes.

Technology

Technology

O is one of the most technically advanced shows you'll ever see, but you won't see the technology. Like all of Cirque de Soliel's® works, the staging, timing, rigging, lighting, and music is a technological masterpiece—like a true work of theater. However, the audience is only aware of the performers, the story, and the spectacle. Even more than other performances from Cirque du Soliel (such as *Mystère*® featured on page 280), *O*™ breaks new ground since the entire performance happens in, above, under, and around water.

At times, it seems like the water itself is yet another character, changing colors with the moods of the sets and music. It transforms magically from solid to liquid so subtly that the audience is unclear as to what is solid and what is not.

O is only made possible through a specially designed theater that allows the directors to control all aspects of the climate—in the water, on and behind the stage, and throughout the audience. The water needs to be maintained at a temperature of 88° for the performers to feel comfortable, and their costumes need to shed water immediately in order to look dry again and to allow easy movement. However, the audience is comfortable at a standard room temperature of 72° and it would be disastrous for condensation or other moisture to form in the theater. These needs led to the creation of a sophisticated environmental system with ducts under almost every seat, and can control the ambient environment so precisely that if the producers wanted to they could form rain clouds above the seats and move them around in the theater.

None of this, of course, is visible to the audience and this is why *O* seems so magical. Performers emerge out of the water seemingly from nowhere. Others retreat into the water and are not seen resurfacing. They are helped by scuba divers hidden at the bottom, who are exposed only for one moment as they flop about like fish out of water. Even this purposeful exposure of the technology and process is handled as a humorous metaphor, as well as a nod to the tip of the technological iceberg that is used to create such magic for people.

O

Cirque du Soleil
Bellagio Hotel, Las Vegas, NV

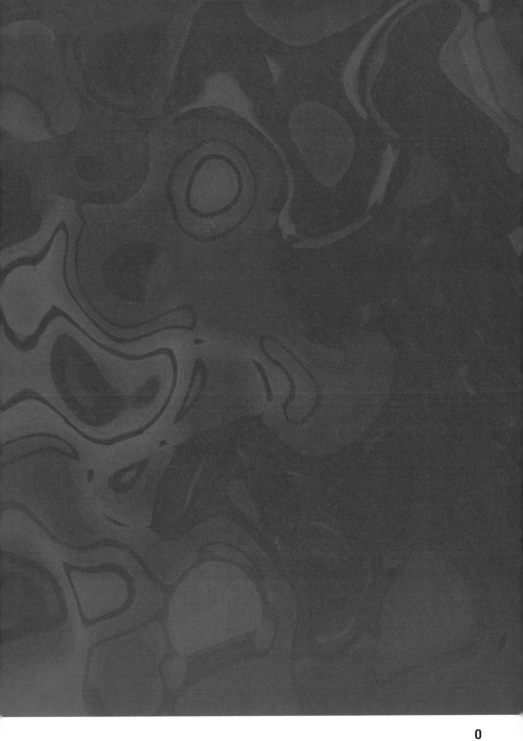

0

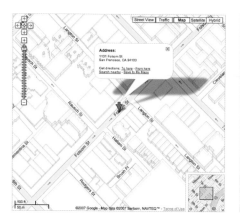 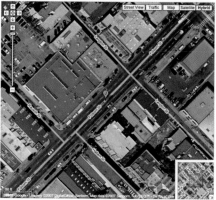

Of the many online map suites and technologies, Google Maps has been a constant innovator and a source of original and uncommonly effective interfaces to map data. For sure, it wasn't the first such site, but trough it's integration of satellite imagery, street maps with building details, and it's exemplary implementation of street-level photography, its use is more clear and easy than all of the others.

For example, its use of a little man icon that appears as part of "Street View," makes it easy for people to pin-point exactly which section of street to show photos for. By using overlays, both the map and the man are easily dragged to pan the scene or move the view. Scaling is fantastically fluid. The man also makes it easy to track where the view is centered. Evidence of the carefully crafted and considered experience are small details like the man icon "flying" when dragged. Another detail includes subtle drop-shadows under address blurbs.

Within the "Street View" window, arrows allow the viewer to turn to either side to zoom in on store facades, "walk" up or down the street at near eye-level, and turn onto connecting streets at intersections. In this way, the view becomes more of an augmented reality than merely a diagrammatic metaphor.

Key to the success of this system, Google Maps is fast in responding to pans of the maps or switching between the various map types. This encourages exploration and helps users find what they're looking for—especially with the often disorienting satellite maps.

Google Maps

maps.google.com

Interactivity is nothing new.

People have been interacting for as long as they've existed. What *is* new is that we consider it possible for computers to be interactive—that is, people can truly interact with computers and related technologies, rather than just use them.

Interactivity is not so much a definable thing so as it is a nebulous concept. It is a spectrum from passive to interactive; and, there's no distinct point along the continuum where an experience switches from passive to active to interactive. In fact, it's probably only possible to compare experiences as being more or less interactive, rather than interactive in and of themselves.

In an interactive medium, it would seem that interactivity would be important, but the issues over the past years have revolved around almost everything *but* interaction: content, technology, bandwidth, connectivity, politics, security, and so on. Even those who claim to understand interaction usually produce merely dynamic media (such as animation) rather than turly interactive experiences.

Interactivity is *the* differentiable advantage of interactive media.

<<<passive

We have had multimedia for a long time (in print and television, for example), but what is different now is **interactivity**. Technologies are not inherently or automatically interactive. They must be made so through a careful development process that makes a place for the audience (users) to take part in the action. Products and experiences in these media that aren't truly interactive won't be successful because the medium isn't being used to its advantage, for example, using the interactive media to broadcast content or recreate traditional passive media experiences like television. Television will always be better at being television than the Web or any other interactive media, though it may evolve onlineand redefine what we consider "television" to be.

The biggest problem with the term *interactive* is that it has been misused by too many companies and people, as the term has been generally accepted as meaning either animation (which is an old passive medium), or anything that appears on a computer or on the Web since these are "interactive media." Unfortunately, these definitions are not only incorrect but misguided in how narrowly they look at activities. Interactivity encompasses everything that we do, not just that which we do on or with computers. In fact, most interactive experiences in our lives have nothing to do with technology. Playing sports or other games, hobbies, and work are more interactive than computers have been able to address. Probably the most interactive experiences in your life will be great conversations.

What's important to understand is that **everyone already creates interactions** for themselves and others, we just don't think about it. However, we already know a

Interactivity

interaction: a cyclic process in which two actors
alternately listen, think, and speak. -Chris Crawford

Understanding Interactivity
www.erasmatazz.com/book.html

control

creativity

interactive >>>

great deal about interactivity from which we can draw experience,
processes, and techniques for creating computer-based
interactivity.

productivity

Interactivity is also comprised of many other attributes. Some of
these include feedback, control, creativity, adaptivity, productivity,
communications, and so forth. Many of these attributes are also
valuable experiences (certainly creativity and productivity); and,
correspondingly, interactive experiences that contain these
attributes are highly valued when designed well. Interactivity
isn't necessarily better, but it usually does correspond with higher
involvement by an audience.

communications

On a philosophical level, **interaction** is a process of continual
action and **reaction** between two parties (whether living or
machine). It is debatable whether or not a computer is capable
of actually initiating action rather than merely reacting through
its programming. This controversy about action and initiation is
one of the deepest issues for interactivity, and may represent
one of the key differences between animals (including humans)
and machines. As we continue to explore this issue, the answers
we find may guide us in creating experiences that are more
interactive and successful than what has been created to date.

adaptivity

Interactivity

The Actimates were the first stuffed animals (or plush toys) that interacted with children, both directly through physical contact as well as through the computer (when its CD-ROM was inserted). The result of these simple, yet prophetic features is that a magical character seems so responsive that it's hard for children not to regard it as alive—at least in some way.

The Barney Actimate satisfies many of the characteristics that make a device seem interactive. It is very responsive—especially to touch (like squeezing its hands or covering its eyes)—and it can be used to play games and sing both alone and in conjunction with the CD-ROM. What's truly remarkable about the Actimates is that they seem so much more aware of their surroundings than other toys. Via a wireless transmitter and receiver (radio frequency), it can tell which part of the CD-ROM game is active and sing along with kids perfectly in sync, as well as play along with the games as an independent player.

Surely, these toys will only grow more sophisticated, but this is one of the ground-breaking products that will have paved the way.

Barney Actimate   Microsoft Actimates

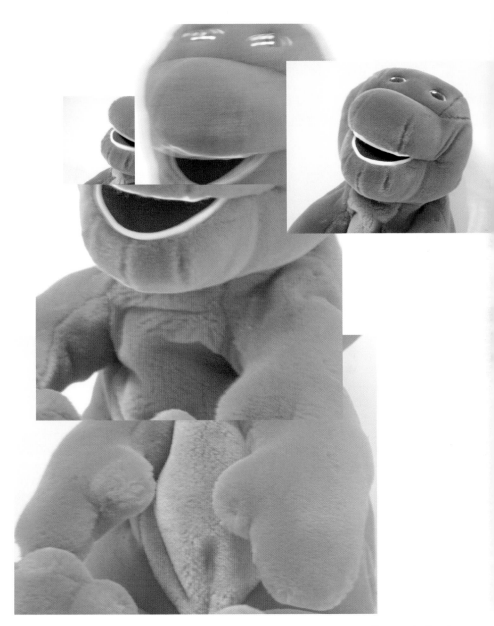

Barney Actimate

One of the most interesting aspects of the Internet is the explosion of webcams around the world. Cameras are increasingly pointed at people, at work, and at the home; they are even pointed at dogs, famous vistas or places, as well as objects such as vending and coffee machines. There are several services for chatting with others visually (basically, the realization of the video phone) and, of course, lots of live pornography online.

EarthCam is a site that attempts to link to every webcam pointed at a place or object. Just about every major city in the world has at least one camera pointed somewhere 24 hours a day, and this site will help you find it. There are probably as many reasons to use the site as there are cameras. Some people want to check the weather before they travel, others want to see a familiar sight from their home. Others use it as a form of virtual travel; if they can't be in Hawaii right now, at least the can get a quick reminder or view of the sunset.

Most aren't terribly interactive (since all you can do is view what's being filmed), but some actually allow viewers to control the camera, rotating it to see different perspectives. Nonetheless, their lack of interactivity doesn't make them unsatisfying experiences—particularly since the expectations for interactivity are already low.

Earthcam

www.earthcam.com

Earthcam

Designers are often afraid of what their audiences or users or customers may do with their designs. If possible, most designers would love to prevent audiences from changing (or "ruining," in their minds) their designs—whether they are designing products, experiences, books, or websites. Other designers welcome audience participation in order to understand how well the solution works, and whether it improves with use, like a good wine does with age.

Participation creates a sense of ownership, which is critical when you desire deep interaction from your audience. It is an essential ingredient, in fact, of creating community. Many "online communities" in the late 1990s, for example, were conceived of as merely passive experiences where "members" could view and (somewhat) interact with pre-created content. Even current, popular forms of online interactions, such as blogs, are mostly read-only. Their only possible participation is in adding tags or comments. This isn't bad but it holds the audience at arms-length from the experiences. Participation is mandatory if you want people to care about the content, product, service, or experience you're offering them.

Experience designers must regard their audiences as active participants— not passive viewers. Many real-space experiences (such as parties and other events versus art displays or theater) require participation *in order* to be successful. These are often the most satisfying experiences for us.

While *participant* is probably the best word to describe your audience for such interactions, any instance where *customer, user, actor,* or *consumer* is used, you should regard them in the same way.

Participants

photograph: Laurie Blavin

Participants

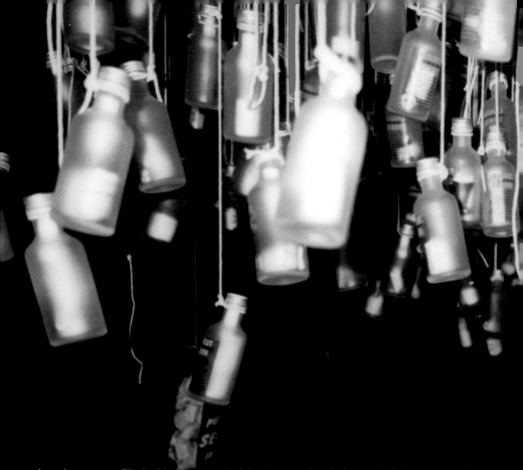

Imagine a room filled with messages left by the people who've visited the room, which were wrapped and sealed into thousands of little bottles. Aside from the metaphor, the room itself was beautiful and mysterious.

The Museum Of... isn't so much a museum as it is an installation space. Each installation explores a different theme that allows the audience to explore aspects of themselves, their feelings, their ideals, and their experiences. The Museum Of Me opened in 1999 for four months, and challenged people to participate with the environment. The audience could leave behind either the artifacts of their own participation or keep them as a reminder of their experience. In these exhibits, the audience participates not only in the experience, but in the creation of the space. As more and more people interact, the artifacts grow and the evidence left behind changes the nature of the exhibit. This isn't, however, an exhibit of audience participation only. The concepts, environments, challenges, and artifacts were all created by the museum staff. They were created in such a way that the audience could not only interact with, but also add to, the experience for others.

Museum of Me

At the beginning of the exhibit, each participant is given an empty soup can and a partitioned sheet of paper for responses in different rooms of the exhibit. Each room prompts participants to think about their identities and what's important to them. Each response can be left in the room (such as tying a dream to a white balloon and letting it float to the ceiling after lying on a white bed thinking about your dreams), or saved in the can to be sealed at the end of the experience, and then included in a time capsule.

Most of the messages aren't visible to subsequent participants, but many are. This serves as a kind of one-way sharing between participants, and spurs further participation.

photographs:
copyright 2000 Laurie Blavin

Museum of Me

WIKIPEDIA

English
The Free Encyclopedia
2 076 000+ articles

Deutsch
Die freie Enzyklopädie
661 000+ Artikel

Français
L'encyclopédie libre
578 000+ articles

Polski
Wolna encyklopedia
438 000+ hasel

日本語
フリー百科事典
431 000+ 記事

Nederlands
De vrije encyclopedie
376 000+ artikelen

Italiano
L'enciclopedia libera
367 000+ voci

Português
A enciclopédia livre
336 000+ artigos

Español
La enciclopedia libre
295 000+ artículos

Svenska
Den fria encyklopedin
259 000+ artiklar

search · suche · rechercher · szukaj · 検索 · zoeken
ricerca · busca · buscar · sök · поиск · søk · haku · suk

English

100 000+
Deutsch · English · Español · Français · Italiano · Nederlands · 日本語 · Norsk (bokmål) · Polski · Português · Русский · Suomi · Svenska · Volapük · 中文

10 000+
العربية · Azərbaycan / آذربایجان دیلی · · · · · · Bosanski · Brezhoneg · Български · Català · Česky · Cymraeg · Dansk · Eesti · Ελληνικά · Simple English · Esperanto · Euskara · فارسی · Galego · 한국어 · हिन्दी · Hrvatski · Ido · Bahasa Indonesia · Íslenska · עברית · Basa Jawa · ಕನ್ನಡ · Kurdî · کوردی · Latina · Latviešu · Lëtzebuergesch · Lietuvių · Lumbaart · Magyar · Македонски · मराठी · Bahasa Melayu · नेपाल भाषा · Norsk (nynorsk) · Nnapulitano · Occitan · Piemontèis · Plattdüütsch · Română · Shqip · Sicilianu · Sinugboanon · Slovenčina · Slovenščina · Српски · Srpskohrvatski / Српскохрватски · Basa Sunda · Tagalog · தமிழ் · ภาษาไทย · ไทย · Türkçe · Українська · Tiếng Việt

1 000+
Afrikaans · Alemannisch · অসমীয়া · Aragonés · Arpitan · Asturianu · Kreyòl Ayisyen · Bân-lâm-gú · Basa Banyumasan · Беларуская (Акадэмічная · Тарашкевіца) · भोजपुरी · Boarisch · Corsu · Чӑваш · Deitsch · ગુજરાતી · Føroyskt · Frysk · Furlan · Gaeilge · Gàidhlig · 古文 / 文言文 · Հայերեն · Hornjoserbsce · Ilokano · Interlingua · Ирон æвзаг · ಕನ್ನಡ · Kapampangan · Kaszëbczi ·

It sometimes takes people awhile before the understand the powerful model that Wikipedia represents—or trust the information in it, but Wikipedia has set the new standard for encyclopedia. The current count of Wikipedia's entries is over 2,000,000 (in English)—and constantly rising! Depending on the language, the number of entries in its database ranges from just a few to over 660,000.

Clearly, this is too much information for one very small organization to create and maintain—so it doesn't. Instead, the Wiki model is that the audience becomes the writers and editors, not merely the readers. Wikipedia wouldn't exist if it weren't for this model. Even the largest traditional encyclopedia, such as the Encyclopedia Britannica, only contain around 65,000 articles in the printed edition and 500,000 articles in the online edition. The world's information is just too big for any one organization to control—and that's a very good thing.

Participants have always been important to events and interactions but publishing and media were often closed to all but the weakest forms of interaction, especially participation. Interactive media, however, are changing this and responding to people's desire to share what they know—the more personal or obscure, the better.

Wikipedia

www.wikipedia.org

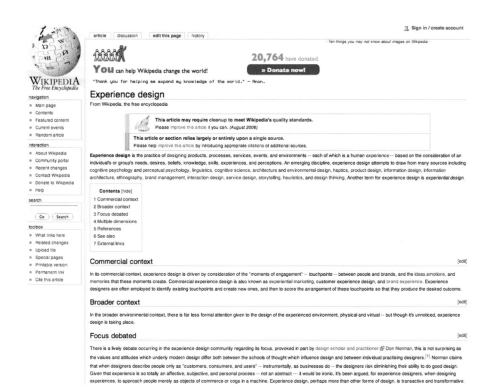

To be sure, this model is not without its problems. Regularly, crises occur where erroneous information—often purposely so—appears on Wikipedia's pages. However, the vast majority of information is often more current, more detailed, and more extensive than from any other source. This is because it's not from any one source. It reflects the shared understanding of anywhere from 2 to 2000 (or even more) people who care about that topic.

This passion about a topic often creates another problem. Though Wikipedia offers guidelines for citing references and posting information, intense disagreements (to put it mildly) arise regularly about the control over a topic's page. Though anyone can edit any entry at any time, edits alert those passionate about the entry to the change, which is often immediately deemed inappropriate or not conforming to the editorial guidelines, and deleted, restoring the original version. These "owners" of an entry often have little or no professional understanding or working knowledge of the topics they care for.

Witness the history of the Wikipedia page for *Experience Design*. Even a cursory stroll through the "history" of edits to the entry uncovers frustration by those trying to expand the entry and add detail and references. This very book has been repeatedly rebuffed and deleted as a resource, despite it being the only book published about the topic itself.

Wikipedia

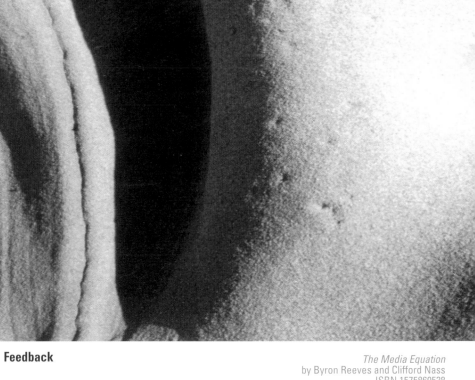

An experience that tells us something about itself tends to feel more interactive than ones that don't. Whether the feedback is a simple explanation about why you are waiting, a reaction to some user action, or a detailed accounting of the system's performance, most people expect experiences to acknowledge their actions in some way. It's important to give just the right amount of feedback because too little may not be helpful or frustrating, and too much may be overbearing and distracting.

If your participants become confused about what's happening, they probably need some feedback to their actions—unless, of course, confusion is the goal of the experience.

Feedback

The Media Equation
by Byron Reeves and Clifford Nass
ISBN 1575860538

Different experiences demand different rates of feedback. Games, for example (whether computer-based or not), require a great deal of feedback to keep the action moving. Relaxing experiences, on the other hand, require very little feedback in order to be successful. When designing experiences, it's always best to keep in mind real-world, physical experiences among people and use these as models for new experiences. Generally, people expect to be treated as they are treated by others, and expect to interact with systems in the same way they interact with people. Cliff Nass and Byron Reeves, authors of The Media Equation, have proved this in their research, so the right amount of feedback in real life is a good measure for the amount of feedback necessary in any other experience.

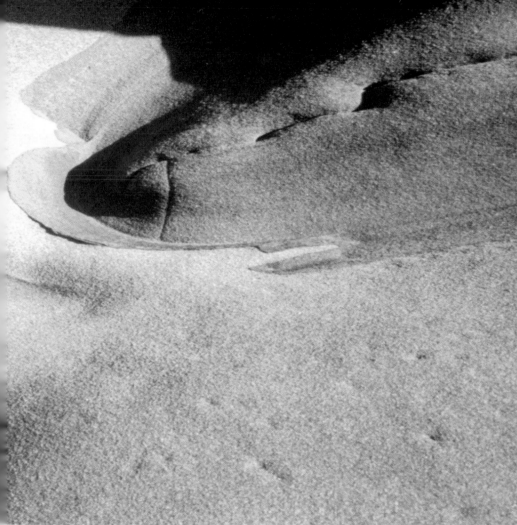

photograph: Laurie Blavin

Feedback

The wooden mirror is a simple and astounding device. Its wooden chips are arranged in a matrix that covers the surface of an octogon. Each wooden chip can rotate independently and is controlled by a computer. Through each angle of rotation, the chips reflect more or less light, turning the whole array of chips into a monochromatic, pixelated matrix.

Under computer control, the image in front of the array (that being the viewer as he or she approaches) is converted, and then played back onto these rather large pixels. The result is an eerie mirror that seems almost alive as it mimics the movements of the viewer, who also is providing the necessary stimulus for its actions. In addition, the sounds of the fast-turning wood chips add an extra and unexpected element to the experience, as it isn't a sound that we would otherwise associate with something digital or even electronic.

This simple feedback machine confronts our expectations about physical media and creates an experience that makes us reconsider what materials other than computer displays can do in our environment. This simple feedback machine confronts our expectations about physical media and creates an experience that makes us reconsider what materials other than computer displays can do in our environment.

Wooden Mirror

creator: Danny Rozin
date: 1999

www.smoothware.com/danny/mirror.html

Wooden Mirror

Eliza is a computer program originally written by Joseph Weizenbaum in 1965. It is a simple program that reacts to what users type by asking additional questions, in the style of a Rogerian psychologist. There are many instances of the program now online but its functionality remains, essentially, the same. Eliza turns statements back into questions following some simple grammatical rules. When stuck, it has a set of stock phrases to throw out in order to keep the conversation going.

Many people mistake this reactive questioning for intelligence, but there is no real intelligence to the program. In fact, it's fairly easy to trip-up the program. (Try making nonsense sentences or changing the subject drastically.) However, when you stick to the rules of the game, Eliza can be disarming and at the same time natural to use. In fact, to Mr. Weizenbaum's initial dismay, many people regard Eliza almost as a real person in whom they can confide.

Ultimately, Eliza is a pretty unfullfilling experience since it doesn't offer any resolution or advice. It's merely a way of talking through problems and eliciting our own thoughts.

Eliza

you can find a version of Eliza at:
www.manifestation.com/neurotoys/eliza.php3

oblem is that I'm not sure whether
quit my job.
blem is that you are not sure
or not to quit your job ?

n to be quite positive.
ally. I'm really upset about this. I'm
y at work/
use you are really upset about this
came to me ?
urse it is.
ou said your problem is that you are
whether or not to quit your job .
don't like my job and I don't know
the patience to stick it out.
sure.
itely.
ure I understand you fully.
my boss is fine but my job has gotten
nd tedious.
you say your boss is fine but your
otten boring and tedious ?
use I like my boss but my job is
e.
t suggest anything else which

>> Of course.
>> What don't you understand?
>> Because you just asked me!
>> Of course it is!
>> Well, you're not really helpi
es that suggest to you
>> That you're not programmed
always is, I think I am not p
>> Because you aren't.
Don't any other reasons come t
>> The fact that you're not offer
Does it please you to believe I a
>> No, in fact it makes me mad.
Are you saying no just to be neg
>> No, I'm saying no because y
me
You are being a bit negative.
>> Well, I wasn't before I starte
Perhaps in your fantasies we w

creator: Joseph Weizenbaum
date: 1965

Eliza

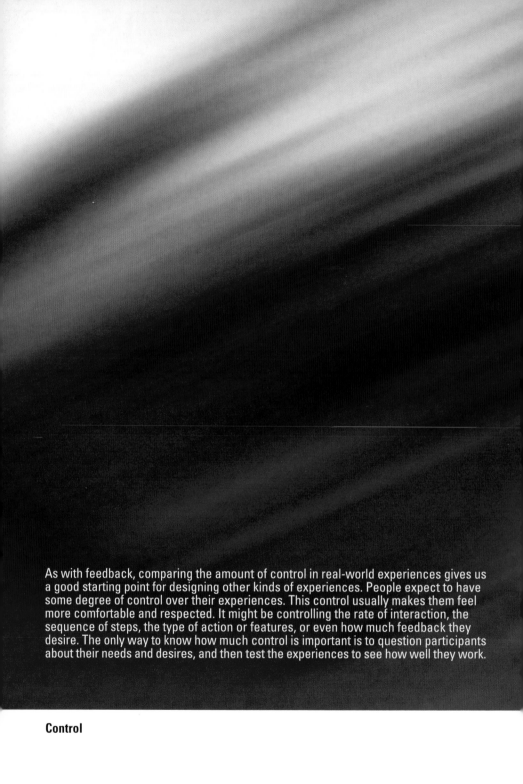

As with feedback, comparing the amount of control in real-world experiences gives us a good starting point for designing other kinds of experiences. People expect to have some degree of control over their experiences. This control usually makes them feel more comfortable and respected. It might be controlling the rate of interaction, the sequence of steps, the type of action or features, or even how much feedback they desire. The only way to know how much control is important is to question participants about their needs and desires, and then test the experiences to see how well they work.

Control

Control

This virtual space is alive with animated characters that interact with the visitor as well as each other to create an interesting, immersive environment. This experience is based on a West African concept about our souls and how they interact with each other (including animals) and our environment. The system provides landscapes to explore, and characters whose behavior depends on how we interact with them. In this way, we can control a bit of the experience, changing it based on how we interact with the landscape and characters. For example, there are characters that only emerge at night, or only if they are approached slowly. Characters interact based on how they've been programmed to regard visitors, objects, actions, or other characters. These interactions occur via sound, gestures, and touch (the control for the experience includes a haptic, force-feedback joystick that allows visitors to feel vibrations that represent the energy of special places).

Creator Rebecca Allen envisions the experience as the exploration of the "soul" within us all—made visible through the system.

The Bush Soul #3

emergence.design.ucla.edu
principal creator: Rebecca Allen
date: 1997

experience design 1.1

programmers and designers: Loren McQuade, Eitan Mendelowitz,
John Ying, Daniel Shiplacoff, Damon Seeley, Karen Yoo, Vanessa
Zuloaga, Jino Ok, Pete Conolly, Josh Nimoy, Mark Mothersbaugh-
Mutato Muzika, Franz Keller, Jay Flood, and Maroun Harb

The Bush Soul #3

In conjunction with the introduction of the first Simpsons movie in the summer of 2007, Burger King launched a website that offered fans the ability to animate themselves in *The Simpson* style. The site allowed fans to upload a photo to be "Simponized" in the series' characteristic style but the reality was that their was very little (if anything) done with the uploaded photo. Instead, the five or six accompanying questions (gender, age, hairstyle, facial hair for men, race, and clothes) directed the system to use an appropriate pre-drawn base image for the "Simpsonized" version of the photo.

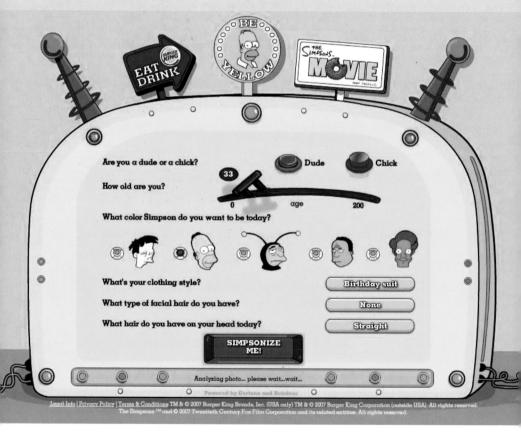

simpsonizeme.com

Project lead, ideation, concept and management: Equity Marketing.com
Visual concept and realization: Crispin Porter + Bogusky : cpbgroup.com
Technical realization: Cortona.de , Facial recognition: Betaface.com
date: 2007

Had the system stopped there, however, it would have been an utter failure as the photos were much too general to be any close likeness to the fan. The animated fanfare around the "conversion" was nothing more than "smoke and mirrors" to give the base drawing revealed a little more relevance.

The real experience didn't start until the customization controls were made available to the user. Over 100 further variations are available for people to tweak the base drawing into a better likeness of themselves. This control over the image, all performed, by hand, by the user is what makes this website fun and relevant. It is the necessary element to create a co-creative, customization experience that allows people to feel like they're part of the *Simpsons* universe.

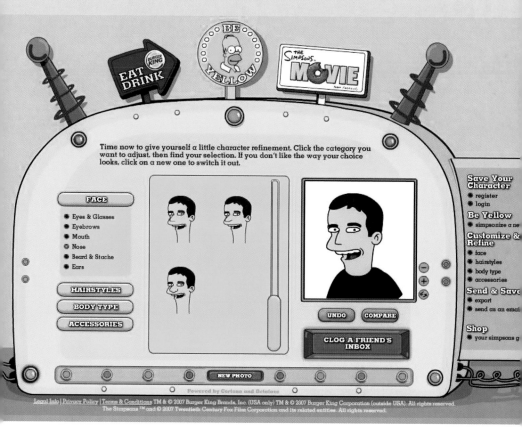

simpsonizeme.com

One attribute that distinguishes us as humans is the ability to create things. While not all of us think of ourselves as creative, we ll create things all the time.

Humans are inherently creative creatures and when we have a chance to create we feel more satisfied and valuable.

In fact, the products of our creation have a great deal of value to us, at least on a personal level.

Unfortunately, our culture tends to convince us that, mostly, we're not good enough to be creative—we can't sing well-enough, we don't know how to paint or write well, our homemade gifts aren't nice enough, and our home-cooked food just doesn't compare. This is mostly true in terms of professional or commercial products. In reality, though, homemade gifts are often valued much more than manufactured ones. Likewise, home-cooked meals can usually beat all but the most expensive store-bought foods, and the products of your imagination have a great deal of value to those who know and love you.

Often, creativity is an end unto itself, whether anyone else ever sees, experiences, or appreciates the output. We feel proud of our own creations—even if we covet them in seclusion. Therefore, experiences which allow us to be creative give us feelings of satisfaction and accomplishment.

To counter our fears and reluctance at being creative, as well as our worries that we may not be good enough, many experiences offer advice to help us make decisions and to feel more confident. **Co-creative** (a term coined by consultant and designer Abbe Don) technologies are those that either offer assistance in the creation process or actually participate in the process by making some of the decisions and handling some of the details for the user. The anxiety that many people can experience when confronted with unfamiliar tools or techniques can be lessened by co-creative techniques such as recommendations, guidelines, advice, online help or actually performing operations for users.

Creativity

Abbe Don: www.abbedon.com

Creativity is often thought of in terms of artistic expression and hobbies, while productivity is most commonly associated with work and value-creation. In truth, there is no difference as each set of activities involves the creation of something. Those who identify primarily with the word *creativity* tend to abhor structure and look upon *work* as a limiting factor to their self-expression. Conversely those more comfortable with the term *productivity* tend to regard it as an efficient and valuable endeavor and are suspicious of "creative types" who, in their eyes, waste time being abstract, unproductive, and frivolous. The truth is that both groups are involved in the same activity whether they perceive it or not. Both find value in spending time creating something.

Creativity

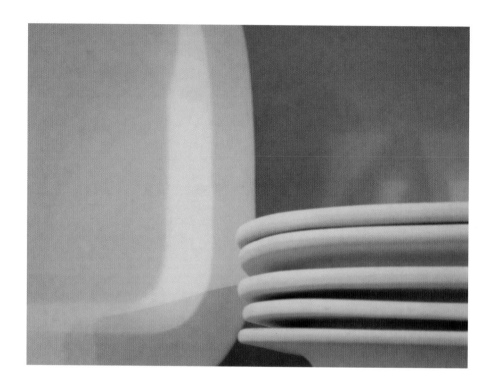

What makes the Terra Mia store so successful for its customers is that the process of creating personal ceramics is streamlined. Everything necessary for painting and decorating pre-made raw ceramics (from pots to plates to dog dishes) is ready for a customer to walk-in off the street and start. While there aren't a lot of variation in forms to use as a canvas (you can imagine the variety if your threw your own pots) there are certainly enough to satisfy most people, and almost anything that can be imagined in terms of painting on the surfaces is still possible.

Terra Mia

1314 Castro Street at 24th Street, San Francisco, CA 94114
TEL 415 642 9911
www.terramia.net

What makes this a valuable experience is that more people can satisfy their creative urges, despite their lack of expertise, and can leave the shop having created an artifact of their handiwork. (The pieces are fired by the store and customers can pick them up when they're ready—usually in a few days.) These are exactly the kind of works that also make valuable gifts, not because of financial value, but the personal value that comes from items created by the giver for the recipient.

Owner Christine Simmons describes how customers who come in timid and unconfident, often leave with not only a newfound hobby but with a new perspective on their own creative abilities. One customer was so inspired that she now paints pottery full-time.

Terra Mia

There isn't anything new about online coloring books. Some of the first toys and visual experiments on the Web allowed people to draw or color. Haring Kids uses the drawings and style of deceased artist Keith Haring, known for his bold, graphic style and unique, quirky imagery. Elsewhere in the site, there's information about the site, the artist, and the Foundation's programs for kids.

Haring Kids allows kids (its target audience) to chose drawings, color, resize, and rotate them, as well as drag them around to form a new drawing. None of this is ground breaking, but it is pretty easy for kids to do. There aren't a lot of options to choose from but, like all design, the challenge is in making something wonderful within the boundaries established. It's actually possible to build complex images from these simple elements.

Haring Kids

www.haringkids.com

Keith Haring Foundation
designers: Riverbed Multimedia (www.riverbed.com)
in collaboration with Daniel Wiener

experience design 1.1

Haring Kids

Productive experiences are so valuable that we spend more money on them—and the tools to perform them—than on almost any other experiences. For example, compare the prices of application software used to create things to the price of games and other entertainment programs (like CD-ROM titles). In the Internet, prices are often even lower—if not for free. This doesn't, necessarily, reflect their value, however.

If you can create opportunities for participants in an experience to make something, it's likely that the participants will both value the experience more and regard any artifacts that they create with fond memories. **Artifacts** aren't always necessary to productive or creative experiences, but they do serve to remind people of their experience and help them relive it. The artifacts themselves often have more than just emotional or mnemonic value.

Productivity

Productivity

Department of the Treasu

Income Tax F
Joint Filers V

Form
1040EZ

Your first name and i

Use
the
IRS
label
here

If a joint return, spou

Home address (numbe

City, town or post offic

Presidential
Campaign(p.12)

Note. Checking
Do you, or sp

Income

Attach
Form(s)
W-2 here.
Enclose, but
do not attach,
any payment.

1   Total wa
should t
W-2 for

2   Taxabl
Form

3   Unem
progr
divid

4   Add
inco

5   Car
Yes

Note. You
must check
Yes or No.

6   St
li

Payments
and tax

7   I

8a
b

9

10
cre

While all forms (tax or otherwise) qualify as productivity tools, the 1040EZ deserves special note. Created by Siegel & Gale, it is a model of clarity. The firm, which specializes in redesigning forms, documents, and other things to be easily understood, reduced the very complex and otherwise confusing process of filing taxes (even for difficult processes like income averaging), into an exceedingly clear, one-page form that nearly anyone could use. Admittedly, its use is limited to the less complicated tax returns and the US Internal Revenue Service never implemented the design in its complete form (they reduced the features to further "simplify" it), it's still a model of clarified productivity.

1040EZ Tax Form

US Government Printing Office: 2000-460-502
United States Department of the Treasury–Internal Revenue Service
www.irs.gov

Your social security number

Last name

and initial   Last name

Spouse's social security number

Apt. no.

u have a P.O. box, see page 12.

ode. If you have a foreign address, see page 12.

You   Spouse

☐ Yes   ☐ No   ☐ Yes   ☐ No

Dollars   Cents

change your tax or reduce your refund.
return, want $3 to go to this fund? ▶

and tips. This
ox 1 of your   1
your W-2 form(s).

he total is over $400, you cannot use   2

npensation, qualified state tuition
and Alaska Permanent Fund   3
e 14).

d 3. This is your **adjusted gross**   4

(or someone else) claim you on their return?
ount   **No.**   If **single**, enter 7,200.00.
rksheet   If **married**, enter 12,950.00. 5
        ☐   See back for explanation.

from line 4. If line 5 is larger than   ▶ 6
This is your **taxable income.**

deral income tax withheld from box 2 of   7
n(s).

me credit (EIC). See page 15.
arned income: enter type and amount below.   8a
                        $

                                                 9

and 8a. These are your **total payments.**

the amount on **line 6 above** to find your tax
table on pages 24–28 of the booklet. Then,   10
by from the table on this line.
by Siegel & Gale

is larger than line 10, subtract line 10 from   11a
   is your **refund.**   ▶

1040EZ Tax Form

One of the primary foci of technology and new media is on productivity. We've heard for decades how computers were supposed to make us more productive and, finally, in the 1990s, proof emerged. But there are still domains where improvement needs to be made, none more prominent than in managing money.

One of the most difficult parts of personal finance is entering the data from myriad sources into one system and tacking both credits and debits (money earned and money spent). In addition, most people don't know what to do with all of this data beyond checking on the bottom line to see if they have money left over or not.

Mint is an interesting solution to these issues because it allows users to automatically link earning and spending from multiple sources (checking account, credit cards, debit cards, etc.) in a secure way so that everything is in one place. It automates a great deal of the tedium of tracking expenses. However, what's truly powerful about the site, is what it allows you to understand about your earning and spending. Not only can it alert

Mint

www.mint.com

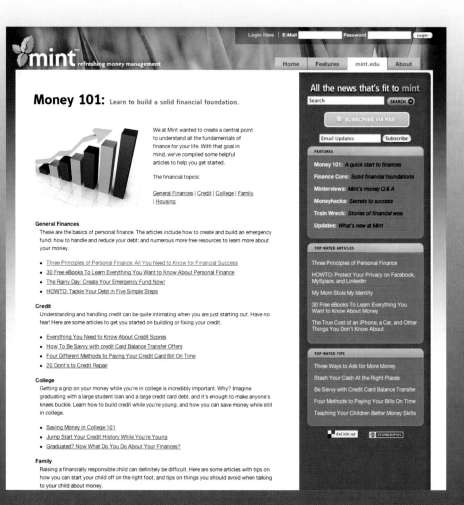

Money 101: Learn to build a solid financial foundation.

We at Mint wanted to create a central point to understand all the fundamentals of finance for your life. With that goal in mind, we've compiled some helpful articles to help you get started.

The financial topics:

General Finances | Credit | College | Family | Housing

General Finances
These are the basics of personal finance. The articles include how to create and build an emergency fund; how to handle and reduce your debt; and numerous more free resources to learn more about your money.

- Three Principles of Personal Finance: All You Need to Know for Financial Success
- 30 Free eBooks To Learn Everything You Want to Know About Personal Finance
- The Rainy Day: Create Your Emergency Fund Now!
- HOWTO: Tackle Your Debt in Five Simple Steps

Credit
Understanding and handling credit can be quite intimating when you are just starting out. Have no fear! Here are some articles to get you started on building or fixing your credit.

- Everything You Need to Know About Credit Scores
- How To Be Savvy with credit Card Balance Transfer Offers
- Four Different Methods to Paying Your Credit Card Bill On Time
- 20 Dont's to Credit Repair

College
Getting a grip on your money while you're in college is incredibly important. Why? Imagine graduating with a large student loan and a large credit card debt, and it's enough to make anyone's knees buckle. Learn how to build credit while you're young, and how you can save money while still in college.

- Saving Money in College 101
- Jump Start Your Credit History While You're Young
- Graduated? Now What Do You Do About Your Finances?

Family
Raising a financially responsible child can definitely be difficult. Here are some articles with tips on how you can start your child off on the right foot, and tips on things you should avoid when talking to your child about money.

users of erroneous charges or fees, unusual spending, bill due dates, low balances, and available credit, it can help users better understand their financial health and whether they're meeting their financial goals. Mint easily allows users to create and track budgets and because everything is tied to one system, it can make it clear when things go overbudget. It even makes suggestions about better interest rates or less expenses services.

Part of the genius of this solution is in having everything in one place. However, more important is the processing and visualization Mint makes available so even those uncomfortable with numbers and money and quickly and clearly see where their money is going and what might be better approaches. It's this processing that is truly the service's added value, much like a financial advisor might suggest the same advice. For sure, it doesn't replace a smart advisor, but it does quickly and easily pick-off the obvious and tedious low-hanging fruit without resorting to hiring an expensive advisor.

Mint

People have an inherent need to express themselves.

Experiences that allow people to communicate with each other or simply to be heard tend to be rewarding, satisfying ones.

There are many different ways to communicate, whether through text, gesture, or speech. The results can be recorded in sound, on paper, as data, or not at all. Communications among people can be monologues, conversations, speeches, presentations, arguments, or discussions between one, two, or among many people. Communications between a person and a machine can be typed, spoken (employing speech recognition and speech synthesis), or gestured (using a variety of input devices like mice). However, machine responses will, most likely, be limited to algorithmic ones within a narrow field of appropriate or possible responses. This is because machines are very unsophisticated, not at all intelligent, and mostly are incapable of dealing with ambiguity—trying to have a conversation with one quickly reveals a computer's conversational limitations.

Like productive and creative experiences, opportunities to meet others, talk with them, and share personal stories and opinions are always viewed as valuable and interesting. Because these experiences involve two or more people, they also inherently involve high levels of control, feedback, and adaptivity. The telephone is an excellent example of a communicative experience, as are chat lines, discussion boards, and cocktail parties. Some of these are so valuable and enjoyable for some people that they have become virtually indispensable.

There are several types of communication, each with distinct strengths and weaknesses: Some are time-synchronized; others are time-shifted. Some are more private than others. However, even taken together, they still do not reach the rich diversity of traditional forms of communication.

Communications

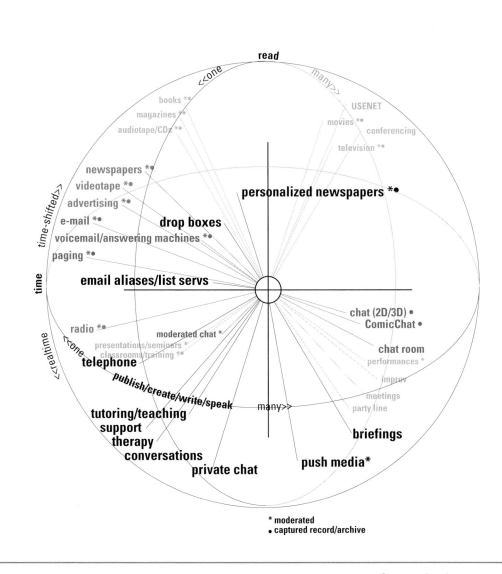

read

<<one   many>>

books *●   USENET
magazines *●   movies *●
audiotape/CDs *●   conferencing
                          television *●

newspapers *●
videotape *●   personalized newspapers *●
advertising *●
e-mail *●
voicemail/answering machines *●
paging *●

time-shifted>>
time

email aliases/list servs

                                    chat (2D/3D) ●
                                    ComicChat ●
radio *●
          moderated chat *   chat room
presentations/seminars *   performances *
classrooms/training *●
<<realtime   improv
<<one   meetings
telephone   party line
     publish/create/write/speak   many>>

tutoring/teaching
support
therapy   briefings
conversations
        private chat   push media*

* moderated
● captured record/archive

Communications

In your life, you will probably never have a more interactive experience than a conversation with someone—especially if he or she is in front of you (as opposed to conversing over the phone or via a computer). The richness of a face-to-face conversation, the gestures, expressions, intonations, and other cues and feedback create opportunities for adaptive interactions.

Conversation

Conversations are one of the most important ways we learn. Conversations allow us to be comfortable and conscious of the content, and to forget the form and means of transmission almost entirely.

Conversation

BLOGGER

AMPHETAMINES FOR YOUR WEBSITE

◄ HOME
► ABOUT
► PRODUCTS
► HOW TO
► DIRECTORY
► SEARCH
► DISCUSS

CREATE YOUR OWN BLOG!

Blogger offers you instant communication power by letting you post your thoughts to the web whenever the urge strikes. **Learn more about it.** Or: [Start Now!]

RECENTLY ▼UPDATED CREATED

THE 10 MOST RECENTLY UPDATED BLOGS

10:52 PM surreally.com
Kalam Kudus Web Log
angelwithoutwing...
Footnotes at
Joelavin.com
Melting Pot
Intenslee Personal
Reese's World
10:51 PM Neural Rot
M O R O N I C.org
Miscellaneous Graffiti

More Fresh Blogs >>>

WHAT'S UP

Media Web Logs For Fun and No Profit: "It's freakin' addictive. So, if you write for a living, don't read this, and don't try the Web-log game. It's too easy, and it will Suck Your Soul Away." We don't like to think of it as sucking your soul away. We like to think of it as giving a little soul to the web. [Thanks for the link GirlHacker!]
– pb [12/7/2000 4:49:00 PM]

Welcome WIRED readers! (Blogger is in the Street Cred section of the January issue.) You can check out our about page for more information about Blogger and weblogs. But the best way to learn is to try it out for yourself. Have fun!
– pb [12/6/2000 8:24:00 PM]

Inc. Magazine's Logging On the Web
– mathowie. [11/30/2000 11:47:45 PM]

O'Reilly Network: 24 Hours With a Wireless Palm Vx: "A copy of the Blogger Wireless Edition was also pre-installed. This innovative PDA app allows you to post and read blogs on your Palm. With the wireless edition, you could literally blog while commuting on public

SIGN IN

If you have a Blogger account, please sign in.

username
password
■ Remember me [?]
[sign in]

Forgot your password?

SIGN UP

If you don't have a Blogger account, sign up!

username
password

BLOG OF THE WEEK

OSIL8

The latest episode of OSIL8 is called

Blogger is an easy way for anyone to quickly start a conversation on their site. Whether the conversation is between site owners and visitors or simply a way to keep a public diary, Blogger is one tool that allows people to manage more complex interactions without reverting to programming themselves.

A blog (or weblog) is nothing more than a linear list of messages. Blogs, now, have become almost ubiquitous on the Internet. They've made it possible for millions of people to more easily express themselves and communicate about their myriad interests.

Blogger

www.blogger.com

creator: Pyra Software: Evan Williams, Meg Hourihan, Paul Bausch, Matt Hamer, Matt Haughey, and Jack Saturn

contact

blog
about
theology
stories
essays
links
current input

archives
dec 00
nov 00
oct 00
sep 00
aug 00
jul 00
jun 00
may 00
apr 00
mar 00

wish list

my norway
travel blog
hjemmenin-
gjaivandt

Search

feel my pain

that's not art—that's just needle...

MYBRAINHURTS

thursday, december 7

▪ Today is the 59th anniversary of the attack on Pearl Harbor. 17:52

▪ Asked of Pete Singer (blogged earlier): "If it resulted in an overall increase in the happiness of morally significant beings, whoever they may be, would you favor the slow, painful torture of professional philosophers, including ethicists?" [via Arts & Letters Daily] 12:09

▪ Grab your chapstick ... Stacey moved her URL. 10:14

▪ Today's Advent Readings—Genesis 1:26-31 & Genesis 3 08:40

wednesday, december 6

▪ What does someone get when they search the web for "girls in pink shoes pictures"? My site, but I'm only the 69th match. 22:34

▪ **ADVENT**

This is the time of the year where we celebrate the birth of Christ, the incarnation of God the Son. Though we're already a week into the month, I'd like to share my own personal devotional readings everyday.

Today's Advent Reading—Isaiah 9:2-6 12:11

tuesday, december 5

▪ Dennis Prager's "Open Letter to Democrats". 15:04

▪ If I had read the official Gore-Lieberman campaign web site more closely, I might have voted for them after all. 13:02

▪ Mullets!

- mulletgods.com
- mulletmadness.com

Experiences that seem to adapt to our interests and behaviors (whether real or merely simulated) always feel more sophisticated and personal. Though these experiences, necessarily, take more energy and planning and are significantly more difficult to accomplish, they are more valuable to their participants.

Customization is one form of adaptivity that allows people to overtly choose options to tailor an experience to their needs and desires. Customization is easier to develop than personalization since the options are always finite and controllable.

Personalization requires a more sophisticated level of interaction and planning, as choices and options cannot always be anticipated. Personalization allows people to create more unique experiences that are adapted even more to their needs and desires.

It is possible for experiences to adapt to participants in a variety of ways. The experience can change based on their interests, needs, goals or desires (stated or inferred from behavior), experience or skill level, the time of day or year, or even location. It's important for designers to understand which attributes will make an experience more successful and valuable to users (which attributes are most appropriate), and balance these with those that are possible to create with the system, resources, budget, or schedule.

For example, many games become more difficult as the player becomes more proficient, constantly challenging the player in new ways. In other systems, content might change to be more detailed or simple based on the point of view, level of proficiency required, or amount of detail inferred from the user's behavior or location (such as a university versus a grade school).

The best experts and most proficient communicators are always adapting their interactions on-the-fly to suit the reactions they perceive in their audiences from body language, statements, answers to questions, and so forth. Because we are accustomed to this kind of behavior from people, it is natural to expect systems to respond in kind.

Adaptivity

photograph: Jeanne Stack

Adaptivity

experience design 1.1

Many fine restaurants claim to customize their food and service to meet the needs of their customers. However, few go to the extent Arun's, a one-of-a-kind restaurant in Chicago, will go. Rather than merely checking to see if its guests have any special dietary needs, the waiters at Arun's ask you about your tastes, and the chef creates a meal just for you, customized with the ingredients you like—well, within reason, of course.

Arun's

4156 N Kedzie Ave, Chicago, IL 60618
TEL 773 539 1909
chicago.citysearch.com/profile?id=3685975

Aside from the custom preparations, the courses themselves are as elaborately decorated and as beautiful as any food I've ever seen—not to mention delicious. In fact, the courses are so exquisite that the restaurant has special containers so that diners can take home the decorations as perishable works of art.

owner and executive chef: Arun Sampanthavivat

Arun's

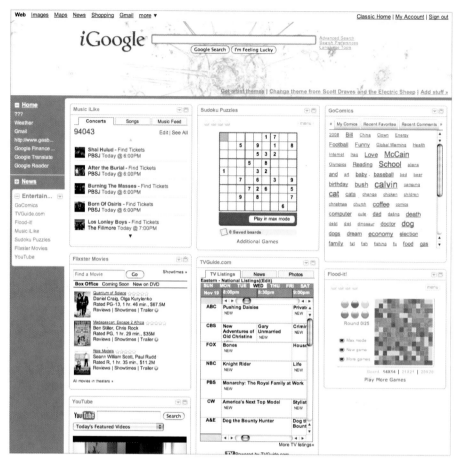

Like other brands of personal start pages, iGoogle is a customizable page that summarizes, in one place, many of the things that might interest you and gives you access to the tools, features, and information that you most use. The more appropriate content and search criteria better reflect your interest.s.

Not only are the pieces of content customizable (if you don't like sports, you don't have to see any), but the layout, colors, and priorities can also be changed to suit individual preferences. In particular, the easy-to-use drag-and-drop "widgets make it easy to arrange the page as you see fit.

While this is a form of customization, and not personalization (since you can only really choose between mostly predetermined options), it is only the beginning of the adaptivity that these services will someday offer.

iGoogle

With all of the attention being given to the creation of online communities, you would think that there would be more successful examples. However, most companies have approached the idea of community as merely another way to sell more products and services, without much regard as to why people would want to be a part of a community. Indeed, most discussions of community show a sad lack of understanding of what a community is, why it's valuable for people, of what is required to build a thriving community. Most importantly, community designers need to realize that the community itself must serve the members of that community first and foremost, rather than sponsoring or supporting company's need to sell products.

The most successful communities excel in at least four considerations...

- **The ability of members to create persistent identities.**
- **Appropriate ways of communicating with others.**
- **Meaningful topics (whether content or context) around which to congregate and interact.**
- **The ability of members to actually share in the creation and expansion of the community, at the very least by helping to generate the content, structure, or experiences in the community.**

Abbe Don, a freelance designer with much experience in creating online communities, adds that a **successful community also requires strong leaders to guide the community and to offer help, to set examples, and establish standards of behavior since emotions are often amplified online.**

These principles underlie the need for communities to be developed over time. Communities cannot be expected to launch into full-blown activity immediately. **All communities, whether online or not, take time to develop their cultures,** and in the process, they change considerably as people leave and join, and the conversation evolves. Anyone interested in creating a community of some kind must be prepared for the length of time it takes for a community to come into its own.

Identity (see page 196) is important because communities require personal involvement, and that requires a sense of personal expression; identity is also important so that there is some persistence in participation. If anyone can say anything under any identity, then no one person's communications are reliable, and there will only be confusion as to who said what. Surely, a meaningful conversation cannot arise under such conditions.

Most importantly, members must feel some **sense of ownership** of the community or they will not participate, care about, or defend the community. This sense of ownership is the most difficult thing for companies and sponsors to come to grips with, as it often requires that they have less than total control over the community and what gets said there. However, organizations that set and enforce clear, fair rules for conduct and trust people to express themselves are almost always pleased with the results.

Community   Abbe Don: www.abbedon.com

This sense of ownership often extends to the creation of key content around which the community congregates. For simple discussion systems, this is obvious because the discussion itself is the content. However, few communities can be successful unless members can, at least, start new topics of conversation, and few can survive merely on the strength of their conversations. Most require some form of content to stimulate discussions. Many successful communities allow their members to create this kind of content in order to provoke conversation. Some physical communities allow their members to help construct the community—even to bring their personal artifacts into the space and leave them there to add familiarity. These are the strongest communities of all and there's no reason why online communities can't achieve the same level of commitment.

Community

While Meetup is a website, the point isn't the Web. Meetup uses the Web purely as an organization tool. Instead, its aim is to get people together, face-to-face, for the purpose of nurturing communities of interest and action. Meetup realizes that we can't lead fufilling lives if we live them only online. Humans have an innate need to gather and interact with each other and doing so around the things that interest us—especially with those in our area—is an effective way of building real community.

Meetup

www.meetup.com

Meetup

One of the most successful communities on the Internet in its day (certainly for young girls), Purple Moon was wildly active despite intentionally making it difficult to communicate. Because parents and site managers were concerned for their young and sometimes vulnerable audience's safety (in light of possible inappropriate adult interactions), the tools with which girls could express themselves were severely limited in their abilities.

Purple Moon's site offered most of what is necessary for a community to develop, including a rudimentary identity tool, and a very simple communications tool (in the form of postcards with optional attachments). While there was no opportunity for user-generated content (the girls could not contribute to the site as a whole), and really no context or topics to spur conversations, what made the site successful was that the girls themselves were so energetic and active that they didn't need the site itself to suggest topics to discuss, or context from which to start conversations.

Purple Moon

In particular, the girls found innovative uses for the postcard since it wasn't really a conversation tool at all. To augment the fact that they could send only small pieces of text a little at a time, they started posting clubs that would meet at specified times, and then they would post the same message to everyone in the group in rapid succession, thereby creating a time-delayed chat system from the simple tools.

The identity tool, also, was purposely limited. Aside from choosing a pseudonym for themselves, girls could only choose between predetermined options to describe themselves. However, this was sufficient enough to meet each other and initiate conversations and interactions. Girls would search for others with similar responses (favorite foods, colors, sports, animals, etc.); these basic attributes were enough to create contact, while the conversations and messages were enough to tie them together.

founder: Brenda Laurel
date launched: 1998

Purple Moon

The creation of identity is one of the most important aspects of our lives—certainly a key part of our personalities. Experiences that allow us to contribute to this creation—or help us form bonds with the creators or other participants—are often more meaningful and memorable.

Authenticity is usually one of the defining characteristics in identity. We tend to discount people we don't feel are "real" or authentic with us. The same goes for companies and organizations. When identities feel forced or otherwise disingenuous, we don't take them as seriously or give them as much respect, nor do we form strong, lasting bonds.

While identity is critical to successful communities, it is also critical to our own self expression. Experiences that allow us to express ourselves are some of the most valuable of all. Personal websites, in particular, are one of the newest forms of personal expression and one of the most powerful.

Identity

Personal expression is something experience designers often fear as they can never be sure exactly what might be expressed. Compounding this, many traditional media companies and pundits look upon personal expression with disdain and deride the attempts people make at expressing themselves simply because of a lack of professional quality. Indeed, personal photo albums, stories, and opinions are often only meant for those we know and not a wider audience, and their level of quality is perfectly appropriate and acceptable—spelling errors and lighting problems included. What's interesting about these attacks is that traditional media find it so threatening; and, indeed, the diverting of our attentions to each others' stories, concerns, and works does use attention that might otherwise be spent on the products of traditional broadcast media. However, serious, quality sources of valuable content have nothing to fear from growth in self expression. Instead, traditional media might take the opportunity to learn from personal media and make their own products more personally meaningful as a result.

Identity

There are a lot of mobile phones (just from Nokia alone). However, Nokia's 3210 was *the* phone throughout Europe and Asia for many years—so much so that it had become nearly ubiquitous. One of the features that made it so successful was its customizability. The covers, sounds, screens, and even keypads could be customized to reflect its onwers identities. There is a huge market in Japan alone for customized rings, as well as a popular and almost maniacal subscription rate to a ring-of-the-day service that doles out new rings everyday.

While many products allow fashion statements (for example, jewelry), the 3210 created identity statements via its changeable appearances—more so than other personal electronics products (such as PDAs, MP3 players, and other mobile phones). Nokia's Xpress-On™ covers are quick and easy to change, allowing the phone to take on any number of styles to make it more personal. Many owners have more than one set of covers, changing them daily, weekly, or for particular events—like we might change clothes. It's easily the most customizable phone ever made.

The small size and cost (it's less expensive than other models and even free with many services) made it affordable for these markets as well. GSM technology (a standard telecommunications technology across Europe and Asia) allowed the phone to roam everywhere *except* the USA without modification; and, the SMS messaging (something only recenmtly widespread in the USA) allows people to quickly send short text messages to each other (now accounting for at least 50 percent of all cell traffic).

Nokia 3210

The 3210 is now discontinued but you can see some of the variations at: www.l8shop.co.uk

Nokia 3210

If you *are* what you're *eat*, then you probably *are* what else you *do*. In particular, if our identities are constructed, partly, by our activities, then tracking our activities (and revealing them to others) would go a long way toward describing who we are.

This is the principle behind Twitter. The site allows you to send short messages, via your phone, Web, etc., and post it to your Twitter page. Every last brilliant thought or banal comment can be easily dispatched to your Twitter log for everyone to see—well, everyone you authorize to see the page.

Twitter

www.twitter.com

 io2

visiting my old 'vegetable' farm in noord 1, amsterdam after 2years. Hehe

less than 20 seconds ago from txt

With Others   Previous

iz in amsterdam till sunday, should any of you dutch people wanna grab a drink - twitter me about 2 hours ago from im

in amsterdam baby - go away! about 3 hours ago from im

3 years n nary a problem with the network until now...i give up 04:39 PM July 12, 2007 from txt

@sheillaellen sorry about that - here it is http://upcoming.yahoo.com/e... 12:22 PM July 12, 2007 from im

Details of xslug july meet on upcoming.org, if u r a regular please help spread the word 11:42 AM July 12, 2007 from txt

otu is finally off to bed 05:02 AM July 12, 2007 from im

In the last 24 hours 'v heard this phrase thrice - "the stone age didn't end because we ran out of stone" - odd that. 10:53 PM July 11, 2007 from txt

out for dinner, back later 06:44 PM July 11, 2007 from im

wonders when @MustangSami is leaving Reading ? 05:32 PM July 11, 2007 from im

hmmmm, tommorris knows psd - small world 05:29 PM July 11, 2007 from im

MacBook Pro care http://www.apple.com/suppor... 03:03 PM July 11, 2007 from im

If anyone knows any intern-age candidates who live in California, would you mind passing this along please http://tinyurl.com/yof89y 02:06 PM July 11, 2007 from web

"I no longer wear a suit to work" - the reason I am considering coming back to facebook ;-) 12:09 PM July 10, 2007 from im

"what if my suit friends meet my t-shirt friends" - the reason i left facebook 12:09 PM July 10, 2007 from im

good night world 02:05 AM July 10, 2007 from im

About
io2

Name: Otu Ekanem
Bio: !human
Location: london, uk
Web: http://rants.ekanem.de
Joined: Nov 21 2006

io2 follows 70 people and 67 people follow io2's updates.

io2 has 52 favorites and has created 854 updates.

Want an account?
Join for Free!
Have an account? Sign in!

It's not clear, yet, how useful this is. For some, it's deeply insightful and they feel that this novel form of communication connects them to others at new level of intimacy. To others, however, it's a bore—trying to make us into small-time, hyper celebrities to our friends, families, and sometimes even strangers.

Mostly, likely, we haven't yet found the right way this experience can fit into our culture and even define who we are in a new way.

Twitter

Participation is the key to many successful experiences—certainly those that are intentionally designed in such a way that they couldn't exist without the participation of their audience. Participation makes experience more meaningful because it taps into our desires to be creative and communicate. Whether we are merely sharing our ideas and opinions or creating and displaying our works of art, it is gratifying to almost everyone to express themselves creatively and work with others to build an experience.

Many experiences couldn't survive—or even exist—without the involvement of their audiences. Most experiences could also be made better by redesigning them to include opportunities for participation on the part of the audience.

Participation on the part of customers, users, or audiences also helps differentiate a product or service and often creates more loyalty to these experiences. Unfortunately, participation needs to be authentic in order to be successful. Asking or allowing people to participate in meaningless ways or then ignoring their contributions can often turn interactors who otherwise feel a part of the action into critics or even denouncers when they find out their involvement was a shame. This often happens in large organizations who only seek to create the appearance of listening to their employees or customers or those experiences geared at children to make them feel involved when they really aren't. In almost all cases, people of all ages can smell the lack of authenticity quickly and if the expectations aren't clear, the phony participation can become a customer relationship liability, rather than a plus.

Participation

photograph: Jeanne Stack

Participation

Now an infamous annual festival in the Nevada desert, Burning Man has managed to keep (for as many changes the festival has gone through over the past 10 years) its most important tenet in place—that is, a time and place primarily for participants, not spectators.

Burning Man only exists because of the participation by nearly all attendees, who create inconceivable spectacles of creative energy and imagination. Walking through the make-shift and temporary streets and among the artworks farther out on the playa, you are enveloped in the imaginations of other people made real. As self-motoring couches and teams of bicyclists roll by, you come to realize what potential we have for outlandishness, originality, weirdness, and fun.

It is the few spectators without spectacle, who haven't bothered to contribute to the experience, who feel out of place in this world turned inside out. Usually, our society is exactly the opposite—we are afraid and uncomfortable to create a scene, to be outlandish, or to portray a character that is neither prepared for us nor pre-approved by the whole. This leads us to consume entertainment and creativity prepared and preprocessed for us by the larger corporate world—often promoted beyond its relevance or importance.

Burning Man is a place that reminds us that we can make our own art, music, and spectacle, and the weight of 30,000 others there for that week prods—if not commands—us to not just stand by and watch.

Burning Man

Black Rock Desert, Nevada, Memorial Day Week/end annually since 1990
originator: Larry Harvey
www.burningman.com

photographs: copyright 1996-1999, Derek Powazek

Burning Man

In-flight experiences have been steadily losing luster in the past few decades. As flying becomes more commonplace and the economics of an airline's business model become more competitive, the in-flight experience for those not in First Class has become pretty terrible. Overbooked seats, less foot room, even worse food (or none at all), and movies of questionable quality conspire to take all of the charm out of flying.

However, there are a few shining examples of airlines looking to compensate for the drudgery travel often entails by improving the experience of those in all of their seats. Virgin America is the latest and probably best example. While some of the features they offer on their planes have been available for several years from some select other carriers, they've raised these features to a new height and added one or two of their own to the mix.

The in-flight experience first took a big leap forward with individual movie screens offering a choice of films and programming in the 90s. Offered mostly on long, international flights, the quality of the visuals was usually vastly better than the projection screens used in Economy class for many years. At least, no one's head was in the way. Things changed for the better again when airlines started offering maps that tracked your progress during the flight and then in-seat gaming debuted in the late 1990s.

Virgin has always had a better approach to programming music, films, and television in their entertainment systems matching quality with quantity. The airline is smart enough to know that these costs are minimum compared to other in-flight costs and have a disproportionately large impact on the flying experience, if only by keeping customers from getting bored or cranky.

In true Virgin style, their new America division uses a custom-developed system, called Red, that offers everything their competitors do (satellite television, pay-per-view movies, music, maps, power in every seat, and gaming) but improves each with an easy-to-use interface, arguably better content, and 21st Century features, such as seat-ordered food and drinks (paid you're your credit card instead of cash) and playlists you can take off the plane when you arrive. In addition, they've added the ability to chat with others on the plane through text-based chat rooms. Talk with the others in your group or flirt with the hottie in 12C, it's exactly the kind of feature that differentiates and extends Virgin's brand appropriately, and it brings an added ability to participate in the flight by meeting others, continuing the conversation, or starting a new one.

The entire Red system is built on Linux and is supported by three servers on board, a CPU in every seat, and Ethernet throughout to wire it all together. This platform creates even more opportunities in the future, like broadband access, new functionality in the interface, and custom games since the foundation is already so robust and its Linux roots allow open-source game and feature development. It's a decidedly contemporary— if not futuristic—approach to a, now, common mode of travel that creates an experience that is anything but mundane.

Virgin America

www.virginamerica.com

Virgin America

Some of the most compelling and involving experiences are organized around the telling of stories—whether from the perspective of experience creators or audience.

Storytelling is one of the oldest experiences and still one of the most powerful because it organizes information in a way that allows us, usually, to draw *personal meaning* and create *knowledge* (see page 48).

There are as many different ways to tell a story as there are storytellers. The two most important characteristics of successful stories are that they are **authentic** (this doesn't mean that they cannot be fictional), and that they are **relevant** to the audience. Additionally, many stories are successful when they can evolve to fit the circumstance and take into account the reaction of the audience. This doesn't mean that the story must be told or created cooperatively (in fact, this form of storytelling can be fun or silly, but isn't usually fulfilling).

Storytelling must take into account **perspective**—whether the story is told from the first person (as something that happened to the storyteller personally), the second person (a difficult perspective to use for most stories), or the third person (a very common perspective).

Most stories require at least a **beginning** (to understand the context), a **middle** (the story itself), and some form of **end** (to draw the story to a satisfactory close and, often, to point out the meaning, moral, or lesson if there is one). These correspond exactly to the dimensions of experience, *Duration* (see page 4). Settings, characters, styles, dramatic purpose, and themes are all important, but without the basis of purpose and flow, no story can be told well.

Innovative experiments in storytelling have tried to incorporate multiple points of view in the telling, offer non-linear or branching stories, or provide improvisational story building. Some of these have been successful, but it takes a particularly skilled storyteller to do these well. More often than not, simple, linear story structures allow storytellers to concentrate on the meaning and emotional content as well as the careful development of action and characters in order to arrive at a satisfying conclusion. Storytelling is so difficult for most people that the less variables they need to control, the more successful the stories they create.

Storytelling

lighting
vivid studios
vivid studios
voice

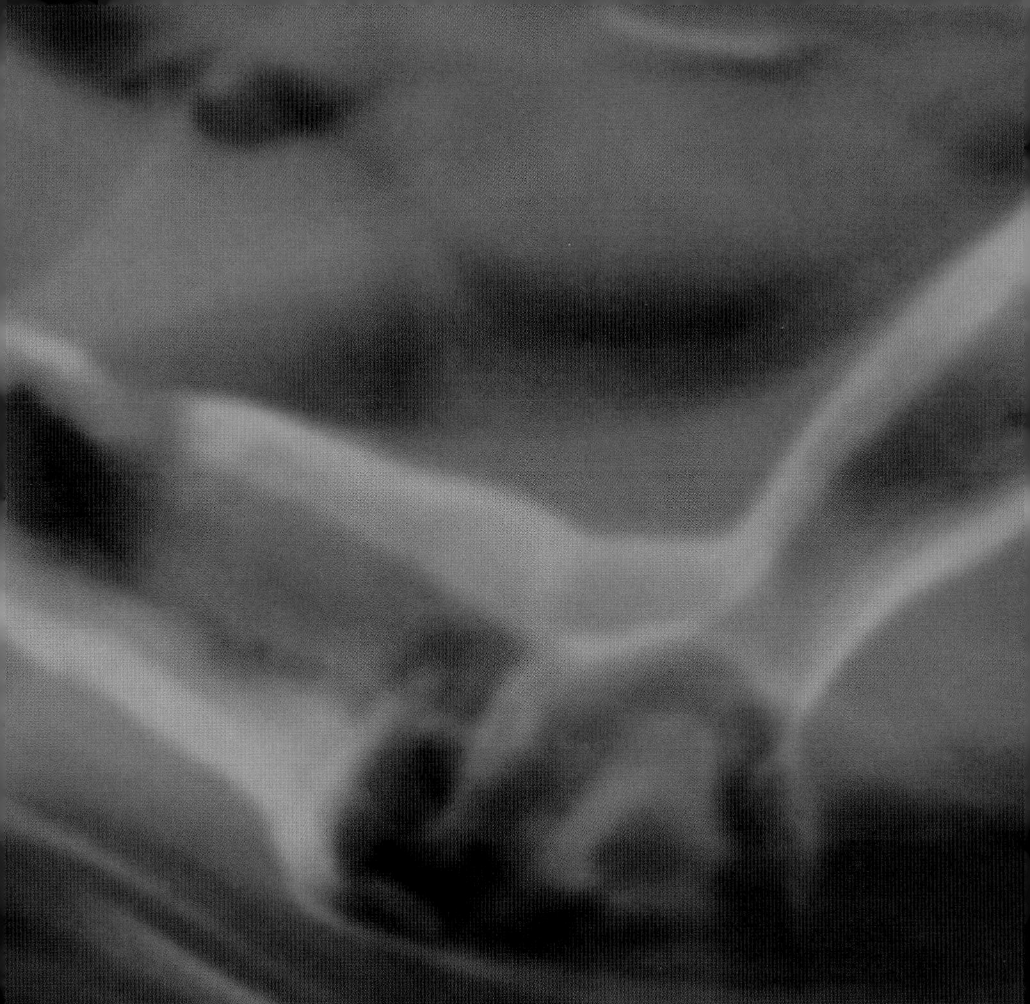

Stories can be used not just as entertainment but as a way to make difficult concepts, information, or instructions more accessible.

Because we are so familiar with stories, the structure allows us to concentrate and order the information more easily than many other forms. As long as the story doesn't get in the way of the purpose or use of the information, there's no reason why stories can't be used to make instructions, directions, reports, or guidelines of any kind more easy to understand and remember. Politicians have been using stories to illustrate their positions for a long time and seem to be using them increasingly for the same reasons.

Storytelling

294
300
300
268

My Grandmother, Myself
by Rosalind Glazer

Grandma Bobbie Green   Rosalind Glazer

I was a colicky baby but Grandma Bobbie alone knew how to get me to stop crying. This was a huge relief to my exhausted mother. She would cradle me in her arms and sing to me in Yiddish. Her father, my great grandfather was a chazzan–and a rabbi–and I still love to sing Jewish songs.

I loved visiting her apartment in Yonkers, NY. Her giant potted plants had marbles and shells which I used to pick out and play with. The carpeted hallways had plastic runners and the living room had plastic couch covers. I can still smell it. The asphalt playground outside her red brick building had the best seesaw around.

As a child I loved her excellent Hungarian kosher cooking, but when she got too tired to cook she took to eating Chinese food and Burger King. My mother told me how grandma taught her to eat shrimp cocktail and lobster. But that was only out of the house.

In My Mother's House
by Liz Rudey

Bertha and daughter Thelma   Thelma c. 1910

My mother, Thelma Barasch was born on January 20, 1907 in New York City. She was the daughter of Bertha Hirschdorfer and Morris Barasch. They lived on East 10th Street accross the street from Tompkins Square Park.

Bertha was born in Milwaukee, Wisconscin in the early 1880's and moved with her family to New York's Lower East Side. Bertha and her half sister Anna Bikel married two Austrian brothers, Morris and Sigmund. The men opened a bank on Delancey Street. Bertha and Morris had five children. (The first died for lack of antibiotics). Thelma often spent time with her Aunt Anna and Uncle Sigmund, and spoke German for the first years of her life. The family moved to Williamsburg where Thelma and her siblings went to school.

Bertha helped her husband in the bank as an accountant. Her exercise included walking over the Williamsburg Bridge each day with a basket of hot lunch for her husband. She

As part of her quest to teach others how to create and share their personal stories using online and interactive media, Abbe Don, an artist and producer, periodically holds Digital Story Bees. These events allow people to discuss the nature of storytelling and identify the most important moments in the stories. Also taught at these events are how to use the tools that are necessary for attendees to tell their stories.

Digital Story Bee   creator: Abbe Don

www.bubbe.com/dsb

story excerpts:

Laura Jacobs, **Tel Aviv**
My grandmother came from a very small town just north of Warsaw, Poland. She once told me the story of why she had poor vision in one eye. When she was a very young child she was quite beautiful and a woman who lived in her village was quite jealous of her good looks. One day my grandmother walked past this women who "cast an evil eye on her" and from that time on she was not able to see clearly in one eye. Even though her mother took her to a Rabbi in the town to "remove the evil eye" this problem persisted all her life. Because of this experience my grandmother never complimented her grandchildren on their

What is a digital story bee?

Well, it's a little something I cooked up in response to people asking me how I do what I do or if I can teach them to do what I do so they can share their stories here at my place, Bubbe's Back Porch. Nothing makes me livel more than seeing people connect with a dormant part of themselves or their past. Ever since I began putting stories on the web I realized there's something about stories that enable us to learn from each other and make a connection between our heads, our hearts and our *kishkes* (that means "guts" more or less) So the Digital Story Bee(tm) is a free, three-hour workshop where people come together with a couple of family photographs and tell each other stories, face to face in a nice circle, a bit like an old quilting bee. Each Digital Story Bee(tm) has a theme to keep everybody on the same page. Then, you shmooz, a little, see a little demonstration of how all this technology works, and follow this four step process:

1. Scan a picture

Each Woman is a Dreamer in Her Time

by Joan Roth

My mother, Clara, like her mother and mother-in-law before her was a dreamer. But few of her dreams, if any, ever came true. She's an inventor. She invented the first hair curler, eye lash curler and portable dish dri, she really did! Even though no one believes her and no one cares, because the one time her hair curler got to the market place, World War II broke out and she couldn't get the material she needed quick enough to produce fast enough.... so the story goes. But I've seen her patents and I believe her. I know she is a genius. A beautiful, gentle woman who gave much too much of herself to others; who never gave up hope; stopped loving those who abused her generousity and never lost her faith in God.

Dora on the other hand was more domineering. Dora was Clara's mother. She was born in New York City, March 24, 1890. The third daughter of ten children, only seven of whom lived. The boys were all educated, of course. Abe, the oldest became a professor. He was the Dean of the night school at Hunter College and is written up in *Who's Who in America*. Louis became a doctor and was noted in the family as the doctor to Irving Berlin's father-in-law. Joseph became a dentist. Both men built their practices in their father's big old house on 189 Mineola Avenue, in Mineola, Long Island. Dora, too, wanted to be a doctor. Realizing she had no chance because," only the boys were being sent to college," she spent the rest of her life wishing she had become a nurse. She did hospital volunteer work and when she turned 70 years old , she was awarded a nurses certificate and a Red Cross pin.

Bertha has always been a mystery to me. She died before I was born, so I never knew her. I don't know if she and my mother liked each other, though I imagine even though they were from different worlds, they share a genuine innocence of being. Bertha was born in the Ukraine, in a village called Tarasha, somewhere around 1860. Her husband came to America first and she had to care for and escape with the children on her own. There was a color photograph of her on everyone's living room table, but no one ever mentioned her. Not my father, nor my aunts and uncle on my father's side. Neither did my zede. Whenever I asked about her, everyone always went shhhh. I never understood the reason for their silence. I don't think there was one.

Clara

Dora.

Grandma Aeschliman
Phyllis Aeschliman Shedroff

Grandma Aeschliman's wedding picture

Grandma Aeschliman was born Lucy Novak in a small town in north central Czechoslovakia. She immigrated as a young child and moved to the midwest (Missouri and Kansas). She married Daniel and had 5 sons by him.

Lucy had taught school in a one room school house before she married. I guess I got my interest in education from her. One of my greatest possessions is a set of the Kansas State Reading Series: Primer to 6th Grade which I was able to purchase some years ago. She had kept a few copies in her attic, along with lots of other books, and I spent a lot of time up there when I visited her on the farm as a young child.

The joke about grandma was that she was very stubborn. She refused to take Social Security because

---

The story bees, like their inspiration, quilting bees, are very social events. They start with a discussion of materials (family photos, stories, and so on). This is where the stories begin to form. Starting with oral storytelling is more natural for people and helps them to focus on the best elements of the stories they have to tell. In essence, the stories are "written" during the discussion so that the production of the story online goes quickly and easily for novices.

---

photographs copyright Abbe Don

Digital Story Bee

The Fray was one of the first websites to allow readers to share their own stories. What sets The Fray apart is its approach to using prepared original stories (written, edited, designed, and produced) as a catalyst to touch people and entice them to share their thoughts and reactions—that is, their own stories—as they relate to the prepared stories.

The first danger of any audience participation is that an audience won't, in fact, participate. Using well-written and well-designed stories as catalysts reduces this danger drastically. Reviewing any of the stories on the site reveals a dizzying number of responses, proving the effectiveness of this technique.

Another danger of audience participation is always the appropriateness of the responses. Often, the audience isn't sufficiently engaged or their motives aren't aligned with the purposes and expectations of the site creators. What works here, is that the topics are personal and emotional enough to be engaging and just long enough to be enveloping. By the time readers get to the end of the story (where their opportunity to participate begins), they're more likely to share their own stories in line with the spirit of the site, rather than change the tone of the experience. There is a kind of subtle peer pressure at work here that helps guide people to be thoughtful and respectful of each other, as well as to be open with their own feelings.

The Fray has been successful in terms of the amount as well as depth of the participation throughout the site. It is one of the best examples of how successful—and how special—personal storytelling can be.

The Fray   designer and creator: Derek Powazek

www.fray.com/index-old.shtml

t haunts me.
ly past lovers. I have
ong memories; picture

ghosts

unted. Sometimes I
take over me as I
ve expereiences in

hope

drugs

The Fray

The structure of a story often affects its experience—especially how it is understood. While the vast majority of narratives (stories, reports, speeches, etc.) follow a simple linear progression (beginning, middle, and end), many of the most engaging stories play with this structure in novel ways. Whether using traditional, improvisational, or "street" theater techniques, structures are a part of the interaction among actors, and between the actors and audience. These interactions stabilize or provide departures for dynamic parts of the action (the characters, the environment, the script, the performance, etc.). Improvisational theater techniques, in particular, play with making these elements dynamic or static in order to explore possibilities, while keeping an interesting narrative building for an audience. Any exploration of theater techniques and narrative structures should explore improvisational techniques, as well as more traditional theater and storytelling techniques.

David Siegel has identified two-goal story structures in many successful books and movies. This narrative device allows the story to change substantially, as the hero—

Narrative Structure

Computers as Theater, Brenda Laurel, Addison-Wesley, 1991
isbn: 081011313

who had been focused on one goal—switches when a larger, more important goal comes to light during the story. This switch provides tension and an opportunity for emotional and dramatic development. Sometimes the goal switches again (to a third goal; though too many switches can become confusing). In other stories, the goal may switch back to the original one (a reversal). Brenda Laurel reminds us that "in theater, perception is more important than reality." That is, whatever the structural changes, the narrative still needs to have a cognitive clarity that people can follow, even if it isn't realistic or accurate.

Brenda also informs us that all narratives require **action** even when there are no characters. Action is what holds our attention and creates meaning. All experiences that strive to be interesting, engaging, entertaining, or informing must be designed to act—even react and interact—on some level. The action is also the best place to start development and design (as opposed to the environment, the characters, or props).

photograph: Jeanne Stack **Narrative Structure**

The presentation and organization of this Holocaust Museum at the Simon Wiesenthal Center in Los Angeles, California is innovative, sensitive, and powerful. The experience uses different points of views (embodied in three characters who represent the design perspectives of the museum) to present the information and build the story, which is brilliantly implemented. The three perspectives represent a historian, an exhibit designer, and a photo editor. The three discuss key issues of the Holocaust experience and explain how the elements of the museum's design help the visitors understand this experience. At one point in the museum, visitors can obtain an identity card that

Holocaust Museum

www.wiesenthal.com

experience design 1.1

describes a real person who experienced the Holocaust. Throughout the museum, in different rooms, there are small machines that read the cards and describe the history of the represented person at that point. It's important to note than many of the people described don't live through the entire holocaust, which makes a personal connection between visitors and victims.

The interactive exhibits in the Museum of Tolerance could be more powerful and engaging, but this museum deserves credit for targeting the subject of tolerance (of many differences and cultures), instead of merely building a shrill memorial.

Holocaust Museum

Comic Chat

research.microsoft.com/vwg/projectsheets/comicchat.htm

principal designers: David Kurlander, Tim Skelly,
and David H. Salesin
date: 1996

Comic Chat

We are mostly familiar with non-linear navigation through our use of hypermedia like the Web, but this is not the first example of such navigation in this medium. There are many common experiences in which we move about non-linearly—that is, where we have choices of how and where to proceed along the way. Driving or walking in a city, for example, are non-linear experiences, as are almost all real-space, physical experiences. There is nothing inherently better about non-linear experiences, though the choice offered, if appropriate, often creates a sense of participation and can be more satisfying.

For many decades—if not longer—non-linear navigation has been a dream of storytellers. These non-linear narratives are experiments that allow the audience to help create the story or, at least, help shape its enfolding. Mostly, these stories have been unsuccessful since the majority of audiences are mostly interested in hearing a compelling story well told than in helping to create what usually becomes a marginal one. Most people don't feel they have the ability to tell stories themselves and, therefore, are reluctant to do so. Also, most storytellers aren't prepared for the explosion of choice and exponential

Non-linear Navigation

Computers as Theater, by Brenda Laurel, Addison-Wesley, 1991
ISBN 081011313

work required with each point that represents a choice in a story, and the elements necessary to weave a consistent, meaningful story with somewhat random choices on the part of the audience.

In her book *Computers as Theater*, Brenda Laurel outlines five basic structures that relate to narrative flow...

• single thread, no choices (traditional linear stories)
• single thread, minor detours
• multiple threads, preset choices
• multiple threads, unprompted choices
• exploratory

It is this last structure, exploratory, that most computer-based storytellers are after— as it is the ideal (or goal) of non-linear navigation; it is also the most difficult to produce because of the infinite choices and combinations. Even multiple threads with preset choices create exponentially more work than single threaded stories.

photograph: Laurie Blavin   **Non-linear Navigation**

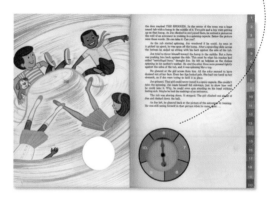

My favorite book as a child was a non-linear narrative that included a spinner that directed the story from page to page. I would spin and read for hours; rereading the same pages but in different sequences. Twenty years later, after learning about non-linear, computer-based narratives, I would still marvel at how simple and successful my experience was using what is generally accepted as a non-interactive medium.

Space Carnival

author: Dr. Lee Mountain
illustrator: Dane Love
copyright 1970 Pictorial Publishers

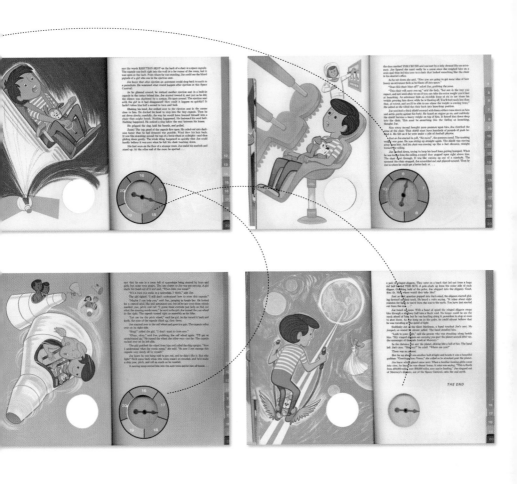

IKEA already offers a website typical of retail sites, in terms of navigation. You'll find categories by room in the house, price, and the other, now, traditional organizations. But, IKEA's site offers several advances on this model. IKEA believes that the best way to sell furniture is in the context of how it will be used. In their stores around the world, you walk through room after room set-up just as they might appear in your house or apartment. Likewise, as much as possible, IKEA's site presents variation after variation of rooms filled with their furniture and accessories, hoping to present something that approximates the style of any single customer.

However, these are not merely photos. In the physical stores, you can walk up to an item and examine it, see the price and it's name, and (often) what material and color options it has. Likewise, online, the photos of IKEA's rooms have little plus signs that signal items that can be examined in more detail (this signal is critical in this context). It approximates the experience in the store in an appropriate way, enabling the same kind of meandering navigation.

Taking this even further, IKEA's special site for their up-market Stockholm line, allows you to zoom around a space, zooming in to see detail, out to move to another item, and offering varied perspectives. While this technique is used more limitedly on the site, it offers a more cohesive—and fun—experience of the same functionality.

IKEA

www.ikea.com

IKEA

One of the most creative experiences you can ever know—or witness—is improvisational theater.

These experiences require actors or participants to develop consistent, cogent, and interesting stories without rehearsing. They must do so immediately and, often, using random (and usually incongruous or ridiculous) elements from the audience. Improv comedians additionally must shape the result into something funny.

Improvisational actors (or **interactors** as Keith Johnstone, one of the leading improvisational theater teachers, defines) must deal with numerous random variables and still create something that audiences find satisfying. While interactors require specific training to perform under these circumstances,

most online experiences must perform similarly—often dealing with random inputs from audiences, and creating a meaningful experience in real time.

Even designers of real-space experiences can learn from the constraints and practices of improvisers to make more interesting experiences for their audiences and participants.

Improvisation

Improv, by Keith Johnstone
isbn: 0878301178

Improvisers tend to view every action or statement as an opportunity (called an **offer**), and it's critical that they use these opportunities to create more opportunities (rather than blocking them) for each other. While this may sound simple, our normal actions (e.g., conversations) often serve to conclude statements and other actions (and therefore end opportunities). Every action, position, movement, or utterance, not only serve to create characters but also serve to continue the possibility of more action. Good improvisers accept offers made by others and learn that the best offers are not forced but assumed. When you design an experience, rather than concentrate on creating offers for your audience, assume that the things they are already doing (see *User Behavior*, page 116) are offers to you to pick up and use.

Experienced interactors reveal characteristics that are critical to all action and storytelling—not just improvisational acting—which they use to make the experience interesting and meaningful. For example, every movement, inflection, question, phrase, and action implies some kind of status or changing of **status** in one of the characteristics of action and interest. Therefore, experiences that allow changes of status—or even force them—among participants, or the experience and the audience, often create interest and tension. The status level of the system or experience in relation to the user or audience is often critical to how the experience is both understood and considered. Finding appropriate ways of resetting these levels can make the difference between a successful experience and a disastrous one.

Improvisation

Theater Sports is a form of improv practiced all over the world like a sporting event—complete with local, regional, national, and even international competitions. Competition is a bit of a strong word for the bout, as the judging is mostly arbitrary and the actors are interested only in the play. If you can imagine tag-team improv, you're pretty close.

Theater Sports has its own set of rules and a collection of formats that mix players into different types of interactions, includes the audience in suggestions (and sometimes action), and varies the experience for all involved. Many troupes around the world teach these forms in classes so that others can join the fun.

If you've never seen improvisational play this fast and frenetic, you might not be able to imagine the experience. Suffice it to say that it is probably the most creative experience you'll ever watch as players try to be quick, funny, and creative, but have only themselves, the audience's reactions, and real-time interactions to rely upon.

Theatersports

Bay Area Theater Sports, director: Kirk Livingston
www.improv.org
www.infotainment.com.au/theatresports

Theatersports

Much has already been written about Second Life, the online, 3D virtual world that is the realization of what Neal Stephenson describes as the *Metaverse* in his ground-breaking book, *Snowcrash.*

Of the many aspects of Second Life that make it worth understanding, is it's ability to create a world where so many people can interact improvisationally so easily. Because Second Life helps control details about avatars and the surrounding world, people are able to concentrate more on *what* they are doing and not as much on *how* they need to make it happen. An avatar simply standing even shifts around naturally mimicking how a person might. There are many ways to animate an avatar, by using gestures built-in or "pose balls" found in different spaces. In addition, built-into the core of Second Life are a host of tools that allow users to build objects, rooms, buildings, furniture, clothes, and places. These tools have created the foundation for the most vast and varied virtual world ever created, as well as enabling an economy of products and

Second Life

www.secondlife.com

services that rivals that of many small nations on Earth. As of the start of 2008, there were more than 12 million residents of Second Life, generating more than US$70 million, placing Second Life ahead of the at least one country's economy, the small island nation of Kiribati.

Because Second Life is a vehicle for communication between people (though not exclusively), it enables open-ended experiences that typify improvisation in life. In addition, the ability to so extensively transform space and identity (each user's avatar is highly customizable) adds to the omnidirectional interactions that virtual world enables. Second Life is, truly, a place—one in which people can explore unlimited roles and experiences and enact new identities and relationships. The rules governing these interactions are, largely, still those that are standard for human-to-human interaction, though there are significant additions (such as flying and teleporting). While there are automated avatars (or "bots"), the emphasis is still on people interacting with others, making the improvisational action that much more fluid and "natural."

Second Life

The perspective of the activity or content in an experience can affect how it is understood. Certainly, the point of view of the experience itself can have an affect on how people interact and relate to it. Consider how immersive computer and video games can be with their (mostly) first-person and second-person perspectives. Stories, movies, and theater also draw us in at different levels based on the perspective from which we view them.

Point of view is also relevant to the content and environment of an experience, in terms of the opinion and context that may be embodied in it. For example, an encyclopedia that offers only one opinion or perspective on a subject might not be seen as balanced and authoritative as one that offers several. Conversely, information and entertainment without a strong perspective often lacks a satisfying value or unique perspective. Experiences that allow the audience to share their experiences can be more satisfying than those that don't, and these viewpoints can deepen understanding.

Point of View

Point of View

At the time of its publication in 1991, the book *Griffin & Sabine* was touted as one of the best book experiences because of its innovative interface, tied to a narrative that supported such an unusual construction. The book was written as a correspondence between two people on opposite sides of the world. They communicate in postcards and letters, and the book's story is this conversation made physical. The postcards were printed directly onto the pages (back and front), and the letters were printed and stuffed

Griffin & Sabine

Griffin & Sabine: An Extraordinary Correspondence
www.chroniclebooks.com

GRYPHON CARDS
41 YEATS AVENUE
LONDON NW3

JUNE 8

Sabine
I am an honourable man (most of the time),and although I could spend this whole
letter asking you more questions.I will hold back,do the right thing and spill
my life story. But it's going to seem awfully dull compared to your colorful
existence. I see what you mean about getting shy...I feel like climbing under
the carpet.
My mother was Italian-Irish,my father Hungarian-Scottish,Iwas born in Dublin,
and when I was one,we moved to England. As you might guess,I wouldn't know my
nationality if it came up and bit me.
We lived off the Holloway Rd.in darkest London. Our s
house was as dismally predictable as the others in th
outside. The inside was slightly different. Our hous
We owned thousands,nay millions of books. They line
and turned the floor into a maze far more complex tha
ruled our lives. They were our demi-gods. Occasiona
enactment of The Battle of Britain in the front roo
flying round like a pair of demented fighter planes
at one another. My father would be wearing his tra
and moth-eaten dressing gown and my mother her lem
My entrance would make no difference to their dogf
accidentally(and inevitably)knocked over a pile o
and unite to examine the extent of the damage.
Life continued in this pleasant vein until the da
newspaper van that thoughtlessly mounted the pave
It sounds heartless,but looking back,I would say
because at 15 I was whisked off to live with my
Devon. Vereker was a potter,and the kindest person I've ever met. The
thing she asked me was whether I wanted to carry on with school or learn to pot.
No one had ever asked me what I wanted to do before. I would have made her my
idol if she'd let me. Instead,I became her apprentice.
Some people find it hard to move from the big city to the country,but for me it
was a piece of cake. Not only did I fall for Vereker,but also for the town of Totnes.
In that green and pleasant land the cider is so strong you have to hold on to
the bar as you drink it. I spent 3 blissful years in Vereker's house quietly
being instructed on how to use my hands and my eyes. Eventually she convinced

P.T.O.

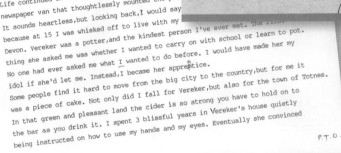

SABINE STROHEM
PO BOX ONE F
KATIE
SICMON ISLANDS
SOUTH PACIFIC

AR AVION
航空郵便

into envelopes attached to the pages. Readers actually open the envelopes and pull-out the letters to read them (and to continue the story), as if they were actually intercepting the communiqués from the two writers.

It would have been easy for this idea to turn into a hollow gimmick. What saved the book and contributed to its success (and those of its two sequels) were the points of view of each writer, used as devices of both orientation and mysterious draw.

written and illustrated by Nick Bantock, 1991
isbn: 0877017883

Griffin & Sabine

imbuktu - sunrise

erusalem - sunrise

Dubrovnik - early evening

BeNowHere is one of the earliest experiments in immersive virtual reality using cinematic techniques instead of computer graphics. The experience allows one person at a time to explore four different sacred sites (Angkor, Jerusalem, Dubrovnik, and Timbuktu) from a central point. These real places are overlapped virtually, and are switched gradually. As well as a geographic change, each place has a temporal change that offers a different view of the site. What makes this project successful is its field-of-vision-filling perspective as much as its cinema-quality resolution.

BeNowHere

www.naimark.net

uktu · afternoon

kor · sunset

ovnik · afternoon

principal designer: Micahel Naimark
first installation: 1995

BeNowHhere

Extending existing narratives in new ways (taking an existing book and making a movie or theme park ride around it, for example) is an increasingly common design problem fraught with many challenges. One of the most difficult is trying to keep some form of consistency in style and tone, even though the medium may change drastically. Of course, each medium has its own strengths and weaknesses, which result in an evolution of the narrative as it takes new forms. The more complex the new experience, and the more challenges involved in creating it, the greater the risk of the new experience reflecting poorly on the original one.

For these reasons, narrative extensions are frequently unsatisfying as they rarely achieve the expectations of the audience. Too often the narrative themes are used merely as patinas over stereotypical experiences. For example, a roller coaster ride tied to a movie narrative is rarely more than an existing ride painted a new color with new signage. While very small children may be swayed with such pale translations, almost everyone else is sophisticated enough to see through such transformations and regard them as cheap and disappointing.

Narrative Extension

More complex is the translation of a theme or story into a restaurant (an increasingly common endeavor). Themed restaurants, like the Rain Forest Café, have some good ideas but usually implement them so poorly as to make them caricatures.

The idea of creating new environments and experiences around existing narratives and themes isn't new nor is it inherently wrong. The problem is that most audiences have grown quite sophisticated in their expectations and will only accept the experience if it feels authentic, inspired, and consistent with the original theme. Experiences that do not make this transition successfully actually run the risk of destroying, or at least hurting, the brand value of the original experience.

Narrative Extension

It is the dream of most brand managers to extend their brands across media into new experiences. However, not all brands lend themselves to all kinds of extensions, and many haven't built the depth or back-story to make the jump to new experiences.

One that has—and somewhat successfully—is the *Star Trek* Experience in Las Vegas. Like many of the other theme attractions that are the mainstay of Las Vegas now, this environment includes entertainment, shops, a museum, and a restaurant. In addition, this attraction is wrapped into a strong fictional narrative that has been established and developed over the past 40 years.

The sets of the *Star Trek* Experience are very well executed as they feel completely compatible with the aesthetic established in the *Star Trek* movies and television series. The shops and restaurant, however, are the least successful—not because of the narrative intrusion, but because the narrative isn't followed. It's obvious that great effort and creativity went into the development of the sets, food, and atmosphere. On the restaurant level, in fact, costumed actors in character interact seemlessly with guests as though the narrative were real. However, the merchandise itself is what pulls visitors out of the narrative experience, selling products that would never have existed in the narrative universe, or presenting some products that would be in many ways inappropriate to the world. Likewise, the food and drinks in the restaurant are tasty and elaborately presented but the menu makes fun of the narrative, and destroys the moment with bad puns and obvious anachronisms.

Star Trek Experience

Las Vegas Hilton, Las Vegas, NV
www.ds9promenade.com

Where the experience shines, however, is the "ride" on the upper level that attempts to pull visitors into a narrative bubble, making it plausible that the visitors have actually entered the 24th-century future of *Star Trek*, taking them on an adventure, and then returning them back to their reality at the conclusion. With the exception of one unfortunate plot mistake, the ride is surprisingly successful and inventively builds its own narrative that bridges both the *Star Trek* narrative and the real world. Though guests *know* that it isn't real, there is nothing in the ride that makes this obvious or spoils the moment.

There have been a few other attempts at these kinds of narrative extensions, in particular the real-time, real-space narrative adventure (the most notable example being the *Alien War* "ride" at Piccadilly in London, now closed). You should expect to see more.

Star Trek Experience

Slash fiction is a well-known, and active form of a larger category of audience participation known as fan fiction. While not new (people have been writing their own versions of their favorite television shows, comics, and movies for as long as these media have been successful), the Internet has given rise to a diaspora of fiction as writers share, critique, and compare their stories online.

Most any popular television show, comic routine, or movie has active audiences writing extended narratives; the science fiction genre being one of the most prolific. Fan fiction is a way for audiences to extend the narratives they enjoy into parts of their lives that the media owners either haven't gotten to or dared to approach. Most fan fiction stories are explorations of the storylines, consequences, and characters in the official stories, but some of it takes relationships among the characters to a new level—often explicitly sexual. Slash fiction (the name is derived from the pairing of two or more characters separated by a slash in the title of the story) has been around for decades, starting surreptitiously in published homemade newsletters, and now residing primarily online. It is believed that the first slash fiction originated with the *Star Trek* characters Captain Kirk and Mr. Spock, who were carrying on a torrid, secret love affair over most of the life of the show—and even today now that the show is in reruns.

Publishers, studios, and other media owners strive for a precarious balance with fan fiction. On the one hand, each story is unofficial and creates alternate, often incompatible realities with ongoing storylines of existing series. On the other, to crack down and try to eliminate these stories would most likely alienate and enrage the very fans who are the most loyal viewers (and therefore customers) of these stories. So far, most studios have simply ignored fan fiction as a harmless addition to the worlds they have created; and, since these stories don't tend to break into the mainstream, it is unlikely that they would somehow compete or ruin the value of the official stories.

Slash and Fan Fiction

for an index of fan fiction, try:
members.aol.com/ksnicholas/fanfic/

Slash and Fan Fiction

We don't always take time to evaluate our own senses and their roles in our lives. Everything we perceive must enter our minds through one of our senses. This becomes so automatic through our growing years that we easily take our senses for granted. However, a deeper understanding (or at least a re-addressing) of our senses can lead us to innovative experiences that allow us and our audiences to experience new reactions to even the most common experiences.

There's some debate about how many senses we have. Many people regard kinesthetic, electromagnetic, and even psychic senses as viable, important senses; while others stick to the traditional five senses: vision, hearing, taste, smell, and touch.

The Senses

A Natural History of the Senses, Diane Ackerman
isbn 0679735666

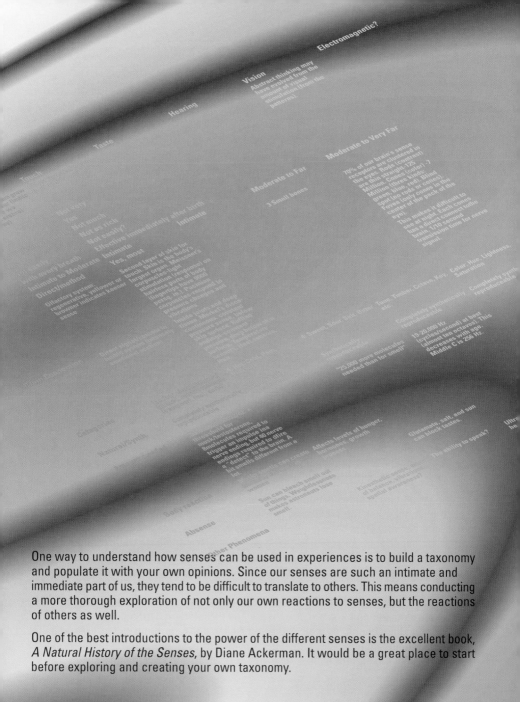

One way to understand how senses can be used in experiences is to build a taxonomy and populate it with your own opinions. Since our senses are such an intimate and immediate part of us, they tend to be difficult to translate to others. This means conducting a more thorough exploration of not only our own reactions to senses, but the reactions of others as well.

One of the best introductions to the power of the different senses is the excellent book, *A Natural History of the Senses*, by Diane Ackerman. It would be a great place to start before exploring and creating your own taxonomy.

photograph: Jeanne Stack

The Senses

Smell is one of those poorly understood and often ignored (at least, publicly) senses—yet it can be one of the most memorable and powerful. Many people speak of memories elicited by a smell long forgotten. Experiences which carefully incorporate smells can add an extra dimension that is both robust and surprising. Shopping mall planners and store owners have long known that different scents can enhance not only the shopping experience (by enticing customers to come inside, or make them feel more comfortable once they are), but can increase sales as well.

Our understanding of smell is undergoing wholesale revision. The traditional (and still prevailing) theory that smell is a biological process based on molecular shape (our nose, supposedly has receptors that identify molecules by shape and then transmit characteristic signals we experience as smell) is giving way to a more accurate theory based on resonant frequency. In Chandler Burr's fascinating 2003 book, *The Emperor of Scent*, he describes scientist Luca Turin's quest for the secret to how our noses differentiate the phenomenal range and complexity of odors. His theory, that organs in our noses capture scent molecules, pass an electrical signal through them, and then read the frequency of vibration, is challenging the shape theory and threatening over a hundred years of calcified scientific thought as well as the multibillion dollar perfume industry's traditional approach to developing new scents. This proves that even our understanding of the most basic of our experiences is always up for revision and new insight.

Smell

The Emperor of Scent, Chandler Burr
isbn 0375759816

Smells act upon a primal part of our brain over which we have little control. Our reactions to smells are more instinctive than any other sense. Pheromones, for example, are said to trigger reactions in our body as well as our mind, often with such subtly that we're hardly even aware of either the stimulus or the reaction—at least at first. Odors can be subtle as well as overt, and they can trigger a variety of reactions that can elicit complex combinations of feelings.

Scientists have already shown that, from only 7 basic odors, most others can be mixed and created, much the same as any color can be broken down to three base colors of light: red, green, and blue. This means that it is possible to create smell "speakers" much like audio speakers to output smell and, in fact, companies have put these devices on the market in the past (such as Digiscent in the late 1990s), but none have yet had commercial success. Unfortunately (or fortunately), it's not likely that these devices will become standard in consumer computers anytime soon, but they still can be used in specialized experiences quite effectively.

Smell

In 1981, when director John Waters wanted to push the boundaries for his latest movie, he created a way to bring the smells from the story directly to his audience. Since many of his camp movies were reminiscent of the low-tech 1950s, he used Scratch-n-Sniff technology to encase nine different odors onto a card handed to members of the audience with their movie tickets. At specific times in the film, a number would flash in the corner indicating the odor to be activated and the smell would be associated with the action in the movie—often to humorous and tasteless effect.

Today, researchers experiment with elaborate theaters with sophisticated hidden technology to create a "realistic" experience that includes the sense of smell, but John Waters accomplished all of this much more easily—and for far less money—exposing the audience to the mechanism, and requiring that they play along.

Odorama

souvenir poster giveaway
movie: *Polyester*

One of the few attempts to create online olfactory experiences, the iSmell is a device that emits scents constructed from seven elemental odors. These scents, in the correct combinations, can simulate any naturally-occurring aroma, allowing a Web page to trigger the device that will create an olfactory experience for any suitably equipped user. Perfume manufacturers are some of the biggest proponents of these devices (which could have a great impact on their ability to sell perfumes and colognes online). Aromatherapists are also interested in the technology for treating people over the Web.

However, there are several potential problems with these devices, aside from the fact that they will be an extra expense that most users will deem unnecessary. Poorly refreshed devices will produce incorrect odors when one or more of their elemental scents are not replenished (much like a color printer running-out of ink in one color catridge). Also, users may find that they aren't happy with many of the smells that are triggered from some websites, and would respond by turning down the volume or even muting it as they would with the speakers in their computers.

It will be a long time, if ever, before these devices are common; until then, there's no way to provide this kind of sensory experience for people.

Digiscents   www.digiscents.com

Digiscents

Like smell, taste is often overlooked as an element of designed experiences. There are currently no artificial devices that can recreate taste, but taste is well understood by professional food laboratories. In real-world experiences, food has long been an important consideration, whether for parties, restaurants, theme parks, movies or even theater. However, aside from nicer restaurants and some parties, food is rarely integrated into the experience—even as an enhancement. Rather, food is viewed as nourishment or an accompaniment. Finding ways to integrate flavors into an experience requires more originality than any other sense, but the result can be a stronger, more memorable experience for the participants.

Taste

Taste

Any meal or food can qualify as an exceptional taste experience but few take the opportunity to be both delicious and conceptually challenging—or even fun. It was exactly this spirit that led IDEO, a global design firm, to sponsor its own internal design competition using chocolate to see where the creativity of its designers could lead them.

IDEO Chocolates

IDEO chocolate prototypes
www.ideo.com/studies/choco.htm

The results are as unexpected as they are wonderful. One design was for a set of model-like chocolate parts to be assembled in different forms to create different tastes. Another was chocolate stirrers for coffee and tea. A different design used chocolate bolts and nuts for building dessert assemblies of different flavors and materials. There were flowers and cases for exquisite jells, and lots of new ways of presenting and packaging chocolate.

photographs: Beverley Harper
copyright 2000 IDEO

IDEO Chocolates

There are currently no sites that use taste as a part of the online experience. Of course, there are plenty that use taste as a theme, for example blogs about food, cooking, or restaurants. One of the most famous restaurant review websites actually started as a very respected printed guide. What makes Zagat different from other guides is that it focuses solely on restaurants, includes a detailed, multi-part rating system, and uses reviews from restaurant-goers, not just professional reviewers.

Zagat

www.zagat.com

Anyone can contribute to the ratings by reviewing restaurants on the Zagat site. Likewise, a vast array of restaurants are reviewed on the site and they can be easily searched and found. The Zagat guide has always been know for finding great restaurants before they become known. Restaurants like *Picholine* in New York's Upper West Side and *Arun* in Chicago (see page 186) aren't where most people look for great local restaurants, but they appeared on the Zagat radar before most others.

Zagat

The sense of touch is much more prevalent in experiences because it is easier to address, as every experience requires us to touch something. Even personal computers use a mouse, trackpad, or joystick to control the cursor on the screen. While most computer programs make little or no use of this fact, the contact is still there. There are plenty of alternative mice and other input devices that create touch displays for users, transferring information via our hands. This haptic research has been in development for a few decades, yet there are few commercial examples that have been even remotely successful.

More common are physical experiences that make touch a part of the encounter. Petting zoos and touch pools in aquariums, for example, rely mainly on introducing touch to a learning experience that conventionally would use only sight.

Touch

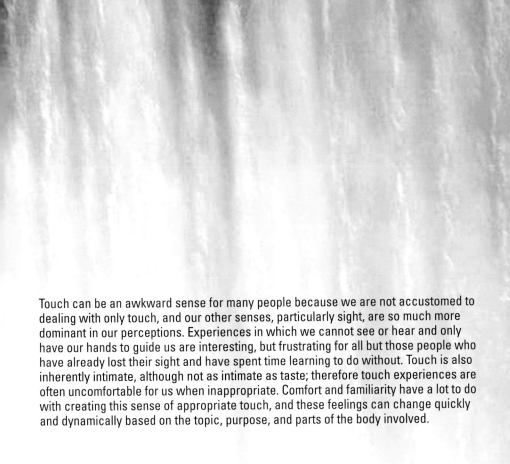

Touch can be an awkward sense for many people because we are not accustomed to dealing with only touch, and our other senses, particularly sight, are so much more dominant in our perceptions. Experiences in which we cannot see or hear and only have our hands to guide us are interesting, but frustrating for all but those people who have already lost their sight and have spent time learning to do without. Touch is also inherently intimate, although not as intimate as taste; therefore touch experiences are often uncomfortable for us when inappropriate. Comfort and familiarity have a lot to do with creating this sense of appropriate touch, and these feelings can change quickly and dynamically based on the topic, purpose, and parts of the body involved.

Touch

The ability to convey touch—especially to transmit it—has been ignored for most of the computer age. Because touch is one of our most important intimate sensations, it can create some controversy or feelings of discomfort when used as part of an electronic experience. Surely the too-boastfull claims of teledildonics (artificial sensation devices for networked sex) make enough people queasy at just the thought of device-mediated touch.

However, IDEO, a global design firm, has built a prototype that shows how wonderful human touch can be by using advanced technologies such as wireless networks.

The Kiss Communicator comes as a pair of devices that are linked only to each other via a wireless network (pick one: cellular, pager, spread-spectrum, it doesn't matter). When one device is activated, perhaps by a gentle blowing across its top or a caress of the surface, the message is sent to the other device where it is received and "played" as a warming of the device and a gentle glow. Though the device doesn't exactly replicate a genuine touch, the symbolic meaning is clearly communicated.

IDEO Kiss

prototype from IDEO

IDEO Kiss

For someone who's never used a Wii game controller, it's difficult to describe how transforming force feedback technology can be. Technology that allows you to "feel" things in the interface has been floating around research labs for decades. A few commercial products have used this technology but never in a low-cost, consumer device—and not for the seemingly "low-brow" purpose of gaming.

While SONY and Microsoft have pushed the envelope (both in technological and pricing terms) of game consoles, no one (except Nintendo, of course) expected that a low-power, low-resolution (at least in comparison) game box could blow by these more sophisticated platforms in terms of sales and popularity. It came as a surprise to the gaming industry, though it shouldn't have to any student of experience.

Gaming is almost always a poor simulation of real life. Though the context of the games can explore themes and experiences that are anything but real, the game play itself has been hopelessly disembodied. We see the same effect in avatar-based worlds, like Second Life). Though movement is an important part of a "world" or game, there is usually no adequate mapping of the movement in the game world to the movement in our own. Mapping body movements to keys on a keyboard or controller lacks a fundamental connection that the Wii reestablishes. This connection is so basic, that players intuitively understand the moment they experience it. There may be other aspects of the interfaces in Wii games they need to learn, but controlling movement isn't one of them.

In addition to tracking movements and mapping them more elegantly to game play, the Wii vibrates and uses tactile signals to give feedback about the game. Again, the mapping is immediately natural, enabling entirely new types of games, and adds to an important, missing component that transforms the game play in ways that higher-resolution graphics, a faster video card, and better sound will never match.

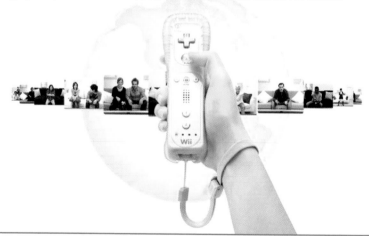

Wii

Wii

Sound is one of the most sophisticated senses we have since we regularly experiment and create innovative displays specifically for our ears. From the time we are very small, our entire world is filled with sounds targeted at stimulating or affecting our behavior. We grow to expect pleasure or annoyance at surprising new sounds as well as established ones.

Like vision, sight is a reaction to certain frequencies of electromagnetic energy (which includes light, x-rays, and microwaves) that our ears are able to interpret. There are certainly sounds (**ultrasonic**) most human ears cannot hear that other animals (like dogs) can hear routinely.

Sound

Sound comes in a variety of forms: voice, music, sound effects, etc., and these can be incredibly complex, rich, and often subtle. Sounds are the primary way most of us receive data, information, and knowledge. While we encounter much of these through reading, still, and increasingly moving visuals, the majority of our understanding comes from hearing. Even visual media, such as television and movies, convey the majority of information through speech and other sounds, and the majority of emotions through music. This isn't to say that there aren't compelling visuals that stimulate our emotions or convey information. However, try turning off the sound on the television and interpret what is happening. You'll most likely find it's more difficult than simply turning off the picture and keeping the sound on (which is, essentially, radio).

Sound

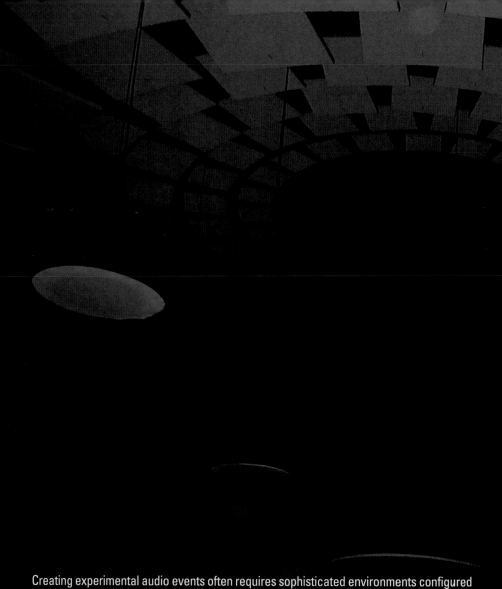

Creating experimental audio events often requires sophisticated environments configured to surround an audience with speakers. The Audium is exactly this kind of experience. For over 20 years, Stan Shaff and Doug McEachern have created and maintained this audio sculpture space in San Francisco.

Audium

1616 Bush Street, San Francisco, CA 94109
TEL 415 771 1616
www.audium.org

The performance takes place in total darkness and the 50-person audience is surrounded by 169 speakers, which are controlled using only analog technology. Ultimately, what the Audium proves is that the environment itself isn't nearly as important as the content itself. Some of the Audium's score is more reminiscent of 70s rock opera and a tired computer synthesizer, while other parts are adept transformations of audio space by juxtaposing different sonic environments, and then morphing the two. Audium's performance succeeds best when using natural sounds and recordings.

creators: Stan Shaff and Doug McEachern
date opened: 1975

Audium

Other than humming, making music is not a natural, easy, or comfortable process for most people. As an intricate and sophisticated endeavor, music can be intimidating. As easy as it is to listen to, "good" music is uncharacteristically difficult to create. However, new tools available make it possible for mere mortals to make interesting, passable, and even satisfying music. To be sure, it's not a replacement for a music education and most novices will not be creating the next original hit, but these tools, like Apple's GarageBand, have significantly reduced the pressure and complication of experimenting with one of society's most beautiful creation.

GarageBand combines many tools into one. Aside from the ability for knowledgeable musicians to play instruments connected to a Macintosh computer and have the music expertly transcribed, its "magic" mode allows anyone to quickly start experimenting with nothing more than the computer keyboard and a mouse or trackpad. Magic mode offers a simple entre for non-musicians to play with multiple instrument tracks, change keys and tempo, and add instruments from an ever-increasing list (including voices).

GarageBand   www.apple.com/garageband

While the amount of complexity presented in multi-track mode can be daunting, it's clear visual interface and easy-to-use controls make it approachable—really, a first in this genre. For professionals, the tools allow an impressive array of fine controls and sophisticated details, enabling them to work in whatever mode is most comfortable. In fact, several musicians are now turning to GarageBand to make the music in their imagination a reality without an entire band—or even a collaborator. For decades, a very few musicians (like Prince) were comfortable playing all or nearly all the instruments on their albums and mixing these themselves. However, more and more musicians (such as Annie Clark/St. Vincent) can now do the same thing using Garageband. With just a Macintosh, they are creating entire albums of rich, detailed, and original music. Garageband (and similar software) isn't going to eliminate collaborations or bands, but it does enable a talented individual a degree of creative freedom and control never before made so easy or inexpensive.

GarageBand

Sight is one of our most precious senses. We use it to guide ourselves and interact with others, to orient ourselves in our world, and to interact with nature. Sight allows nature to convey a great deal of data about itself (weather, time of day, and so on) and we use this data in subtle and often unconscious ways.

Of course, as we experience it, vision is only a small slice of the electromagnetic spectrum and it doesn't even encompass all of the spectrum that is visible. The slice of light that our eyes can see includes a seemingly endless spectrum of **colors** moving from red to violet. Outside of this range, however, light still exists and some animals and many machines can see in these ranges. Bees and other insects can see in the **ultraviolet** and this helps them distinguish among flowers. **Infrared** light is used in most small wireless devices like remote controls. It is also used in night-vision equipment because it allows us to distinguish heat sources (like bodies) and, thus, "see" in the dark.

Because of how our eyesight works, when we design, it is often more important to make our designs work first in grayscale before adding color as our designs will then be clearer and easier for an audience to read (whether human or machine). Black-and-white copiers, for example, see color based on their light values and have a hard time distinguishing light blue from white or dark red from black. Other grayscale sensors have the same problems even though the difference in colors are clear to us.

Sight

Human vision is composed of small rods and cones in our eyes which are sensitive to the spectrum of visible light. The rods are sensitive to the amount of light (allowing us to distinguish light from dark), and the cones are sensitive to frequency of light (allowing us to distinguish colors). We have many more rods than cones, which means that we actually see the amount of light (white, black, and grays) before we see color. While rods give us more and stronger light information, cones enable us to see detail more sharply. Because cones are more prevalent than rods in the fovea (an area at the center of our field of vision), we see more color there than light value. However, we don't perceive any difference in our environment when we use our whole eye because our brains easily integrate the images, even though we aren't seeing in the same way from our center of focus to our peripheral vision.

Our eyes are also attuned to seeing movement, as are most predatory animals (for example cats and birds). This means that experiences that require us to discern small subtle differences or movements are easier for us than distinguishing detail in large, broad sections that are static.

Knowing how the eye sees (and how machines perceive light) can lead us to new experiences that exploit or play with these phenomena in novel ways.

Sight

One of the media controversies in 2000 was a mini-tempest over infrared vision features in SONY video cameras. The fury was over the fact that infrared video (and photos, for that matter) can often make it appear as if you are seeing through clothing. While this isn't really the x-ray vision 1950s advertisers promised (the camera can't actually see visual spectrum light through clothing or any other materials), infrared vision used in the daytime (as opposed to night viewing, which is common in the military) does have the *appearance* of looking at someone's naked silhouette.

SONY NightShot

NightShot™ Infrared vision system available
on some SONY video cameras

The truth is that all CCDs (Charged Coupled Devices are the light-sensing part of an electronic camera) are sensitive to infrared light, however, only SONY products have bothered to enable this part of the spectrum to be recorded. After the controversy arose, SONY disabled the feature for daytime use (a light sensor turns off the feature if it senses daylight), but it's easily defeated by simply covering the sensor.

Rather than concentrating on the *faux* nefarious use, instead we should be experimenting with a new way of seeing and recording images. Many insects and animals can be viewed in the infrared spectrum, and for the first time humans can inexpensively record them in their environments. The experience of seeing in a new way should be an opportunity to see what is new to us.

SONY NightShot

EarthBrowser

Lunar Software
www.earthbrowser.com

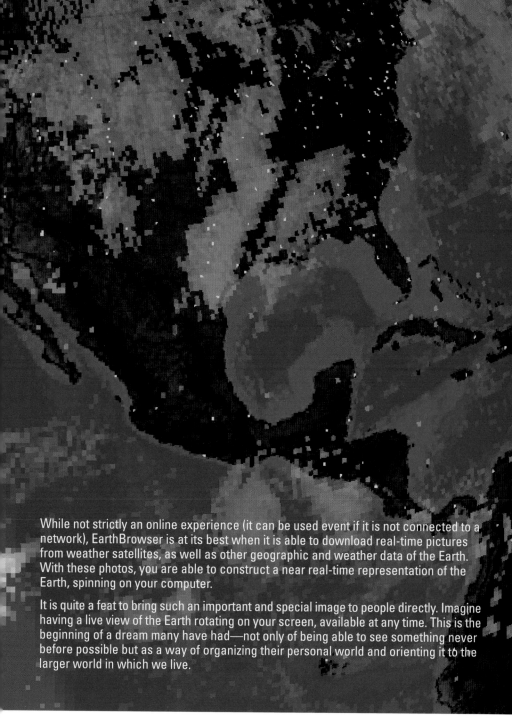

While not strictly an online experience (it can be used event if it is not connected to a network), EarthBrowser is at its best when it is able to download real-time pictures from weather satellites, as well as other geographic and weather data of the Earth. With these photos, you are able to construct a near real-time representation of the Earth, spinning on your computer.

It is quite a feat to bring such an important and special image to people directly. Imagine having a live view of the Earth rotating on your screen, available at any time. This is the beginning of a dream many have had—not only of being able to see something never before possible but as a way of organizing their personal world and orienting it to the larger world in which we live.

creator: Matthew Giger

EarthBrowser

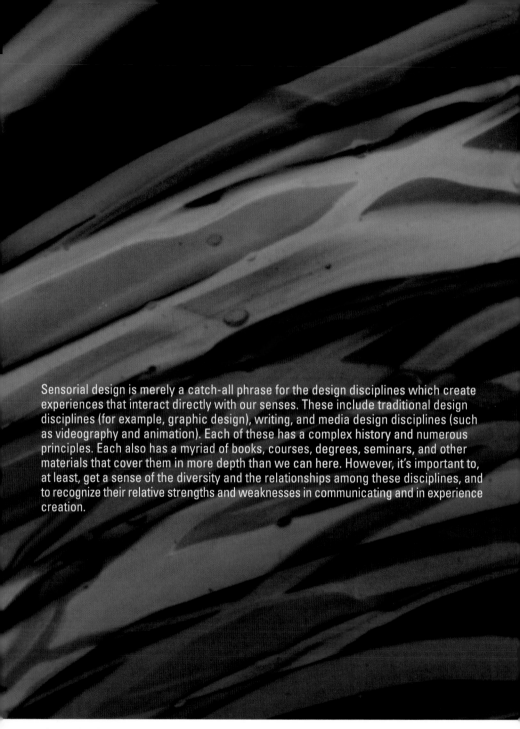

Sensorial design is merely a catch-all phrase for the design disciplines which create experiences that interact directly with our senses. These include traditional design disciplines (for example, graphic design), writing, and media design disciplines (such as videography and animation). Each of these has a complex history and numerous principles. Each also has a myriad of books, courses, degrees, seminars, and other materials that cover them in more depth than we can here. However, it's important to, at least, get a sense of the diversity and the relationships among these disciplines, and to recognize their relative strengths and weaknesses in communicating and in experience creation.

Sensorial Design

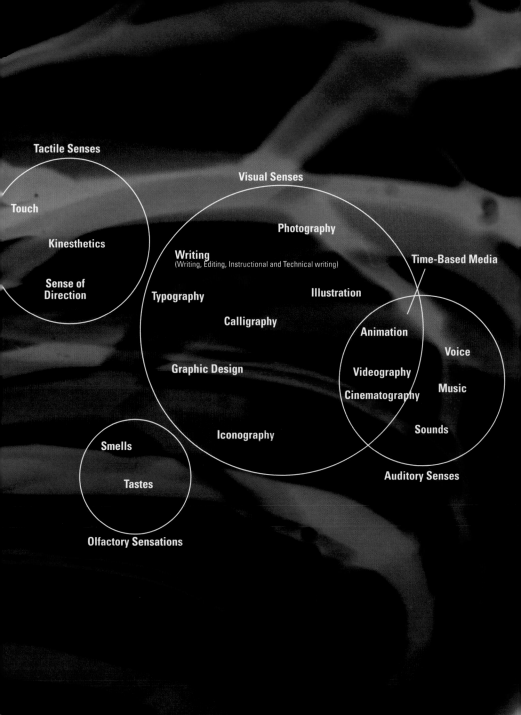

Tactile Senses

Touch

Kinesthetics

Sense of
Direction

Visual Senses

Photography

Writing
(Writing, Editing, Instructional and Technical writing)

Typography

Illustration

Time-Based Media

Calligraphy

Animation

Voice

Graphic Design

Videography

Cinematography

Music

Iconography

Sounds

Smells

Tastes

Auditory Senses

Olfactory Sensations

Sensorial Design

While visual design traditionally has been concerned with appearance, it can communicate more than mere beauty; it can evoke meaning in any decision that builds on visual appearance. In particular, graphic and illustrative **styles** convey cultural cues that help people indentify designs with different values. Though most designers make choices based on what they prefer or what "looks nice" (and, unfortunately, are taught to do so), the best designers choose each element of visual design, including typography, color, layout, and photography based on how they want to communicate the message to the intended audience. The overall design must still feel consistent and clear, and it should certainly be handsome, but great designs communicate first and are beautiful second. Likewise, these designs tend to transcend trends more readily since they build upon a more meaningful and less stylish foundation.

Consider visual attributes not as elements solely of style, but as triggers that evoke different expectations, understanding, and identity with customers and other audiences. These are highly dependent, of course, on cultural understandings. For example, the color white in Western cultures is often used to connote elegance, simplicity, purity, or sophistication. White, however, in Korea and some other Asian cultures is a symbol of death and mourning. Every visual element (for that matter, every sensory element) triggers meaning about the product, service, event, or associated experiences. Understanding design elements as triggers also shifts the choice of these elements form attributes of inspiration, chosen at whim by designers, to deliberate choices of meaning, tested with audiences to ensure that the sum total of the attributes are communicating the intended meaning *from the audience's or customer's perspective*.

Style is difficult to categorize or characterize anyway because different elements will communicate different meanings to different people. Few people have a well-educated understanding of design or a high visual literacy. However, this isn't their fault as much as it's merely a missed opportunity in our society, making it more challenging for designers to construct experiences. As long as designers focus on their audiences and not themselves, they will communicate more successfully.

Visual Design

Visual Design

Cirque du Soleil® is more theater than circus, and where it does overlap with the stereotype of a circus, it is so advanced and elaborate that it seems wholly new and magical. *Mystère,*® one of its most successful productions, makes a standard circus seem more like a series of athletic events than the feats of strength and agility, beauty, and mystery that the Cirque du Soleil performers create. One of the important ways they do this is by creating narratives around the acts, and then weaving them throughout the evening with reoccurring characters. They include the audience on occasion, first making them the butt of the joke, then including them as fellow performers.

Mystère, and most of the Cirque du Soleil productions, are not light-hearted, happy, silly shows. More often than not, they are dark, brooding, emotional, and intense productions.

All interaction aside, the Cirque du Soleil productions are also know for their incredible beauty. Their particular mix of lighting, set design, costumes, and music create a seamless experience that transforms the story and actors into something other-worldly and fantastic. Afterward, the performance seems more like a dream than a memory, and the translucent, multi-dimensional nature of the design, imagery, and activity can take much of the credit.

Mystère

Cirque du Soleil
http://www.cirquedusoleil.com/en/piste/mystere.html

Mystère

【恩源】✚

寻找的终点最终依然是起点

1

johnathan yuen.com

designer: Jonathan Yuen

www.jonathanyeun.com/main.html

experience design 1.1

Little needs to be said about the extraordinarily beautiful interface that gracefully unveils Jonathan Yeun's portfolio of work. It expertly slows-down the user's tempo without aggravation and enfolds a beautiful, harmonious experience that reflects incredibly well on his other work.

【童心】[3]
用中庸的心态来审观一切

jonathanyuen.com

Most designers of digital experiences dream of building an experience so immersive that the participants regard it as all-encompassing and forget that the experience may be artificial or contrived. This is usually accomplished through virtual reality technologies like goggles displaying computer-generated imagery, and headphones often supplying 3D sound. What most designers of these systems fail to understand is that immersive experiences surround us in the real world, and we have well-developed expectations for such experiences. Indeed, our sense of reality is so sensorially stimulating that it's nearly impossible to design an experience that could even approach the immersiveness of reality.

This being the case, it's often a better strategy to build experiences that cannot exist in reality and, therefore, side-track our senses with novelty and originality rather than simulating reality as we have become accustomed to experiencing it. These are the approaches that often make us forget that we are not in our normal worlds.

Immersion does, however, require more than mere novelty. To be an immersive experience (as opposed to just an engrossing one), it needs to stimulate—if not redirect our attention on—our major senses, vision and hearing. Films do this regularly without using any unfamiliar technology. When the story is interesting and the sound and visions capturing, we fall into the experience with rapt attention for the duration. Most people can remember instances where they fall out of such experiences (suddenly remembering they're in a theater, or noticing the people or environment around them). This might be

Immersion

due to the noises of those around us or a disruption in the environment. However, it could result just as easily from a disruption in the narrative, such as anachronistic development or a lapse in consistency or believability.

Thus, immersion is as much a result of the narrative's ability to capture and hold our attention as it is the visuals, audio, or other sensory displays that divert our attention toward the experience. In fact, a good story (whether told aloud or read in a book) can more often immerse us in another world than the most advanced technological systems.

Immersive experiments tend to favor the technological—in which the most attention is paid to technological tricks—than in building a cognitively interesting and consistent experience. These technological tricks usually aim to stimulate our senses in novel ways or build elaborate environments that enclose us.

Theater has always experimented with ways to immerse the audience. The theater tends to create more cognitively cohesive experiences and to experiment with non-digital ways to immerse people. Theater often mixes elements like live actors, sets, recorded and live music, lighting, interaction, sets, and rehearsal more than its digital counterparts. It tends to focus less on interactivity and meaning and more on elaborate, expensive, and digitally-prejudiced solutions to problems—often solving problems much easier, more elegantly, and less disruptively—than with computers.

Immersion

One of the most exciting additions to the *Star Trek* universe was the Holodeck from *Star Trek: The Next Generation*. It's a multi-purpose, immersive, and interactive technology that allows people, places, climate, and sensations to be created from "thin air." This is probably the most recognizable innovation of *Star Trek*, and it has become an archetypal experience, as well as the pinnacle of immersive spaces. Naturally, this is a fantasy and the technology to create such an experience is not likely to be developed—certainly not for a very long time.

However, Debra Solomon, an artist living and working in Amsterdam has taken this concept and insinuated it into her online and offline installations. More than merely a simulation space, the-living has staged events, demonstrations, and four-day improvisations in the various spaces she has constructed. Past installations switched between the Holodeck's recognizable grid lines (made almost psychedelic with new, implied surfaces) and sets of her creation. Visitors were presented an environment that was both familiar and fantastic, recognizable and disorienting, determined and still open to interpretation.

the-living: artist astronaut

artist: Debra Solomon
date: 1999 and continuing

Her installation, the *artist-astronaut* project, not only creates a virtual environment from a physical one, but there is a narrative thread on which participants can create a future scenario concerning artists becoming astronauts. The mission of these astronauts was to interpret the experience and opportunities of space for the rest of humanity. The participants were hypnotized with a constructed, shared history outlining major events, and then were awaken in the year 2035 when they received awards for their achievements as artist-astronauts. The participants then created the rest of the story within this state and described their roles and achievements, outlining what they had accomplished and what they learned from their experiences. The installation was a simulation in both space and story as well as in time.

One outcome of this project has been the creation of an independent agency to integrate artists into the European space program, making the *artist-astronaut* installation a test simulation in yet another form.

the-living: artist astronaut

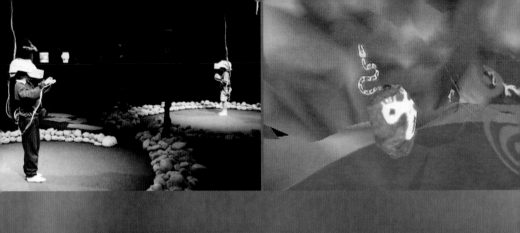

Placeholder is one of the most human, innovative, and successful experiments in virtual reality. Its innovation is in participant movement and control within a system. In particular, people have not one but two hand controls (with corresponding representations, since we have two hands) that enable them to grasp things. Another innovation is that rather than pointing one's fingers into a gun-like shape and pulling the imaginary trigger as a way of flying through the virtual space (the standard way of "flying" in most VR systems), one does something much more natural and representational: they flap their arms like a bird.

Placeholder has several specialized environments, each offering different objects to play with, and several characters that participants can "capture" and become. When merged with one of the characters, participants temporarily take on their perceptions (for example, a change in visual perception), and their mode of movement (such as a slithering snake). Placeholder is one of the only VR environments that allow participants to change basic perceptions and explore life—or, at least, activity—through these other perspectives.

Placeholder

www.tauzero.com/Brenda_Laurel/Severed_Heads/CGQ_Placeholder.html
principal creators: Brenda Laurel and Rachel Strickland
date launched: 1998

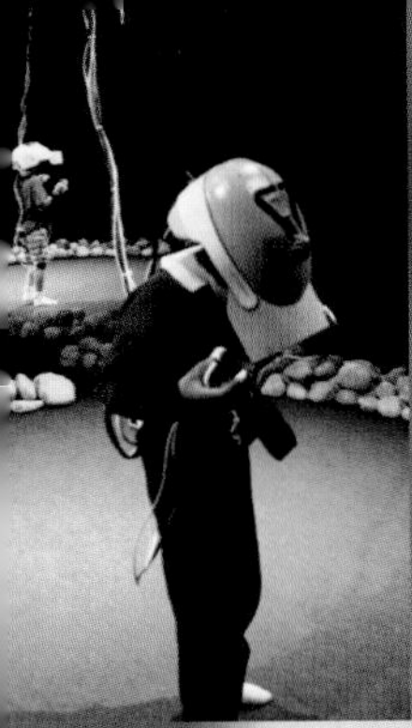
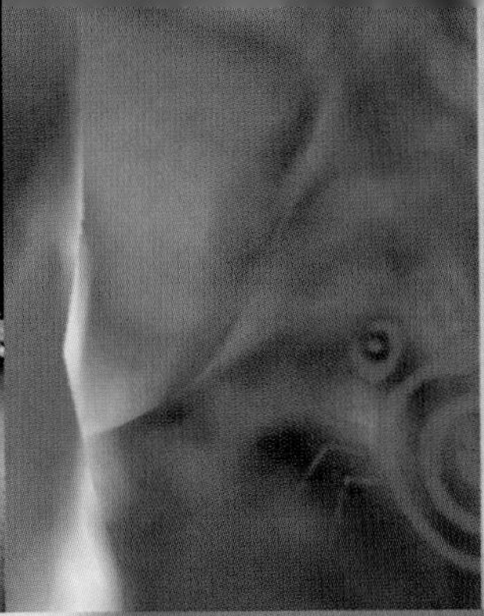
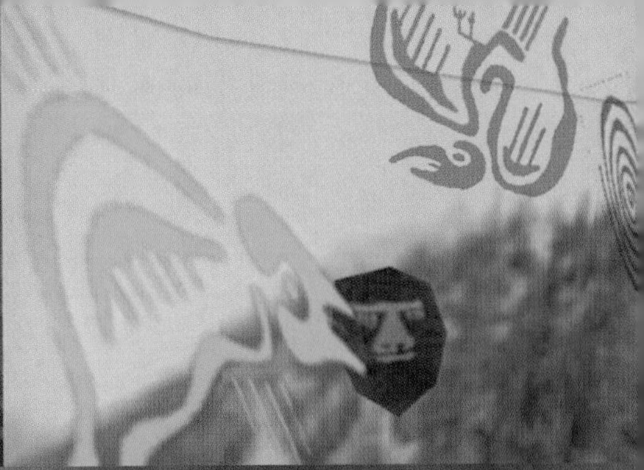
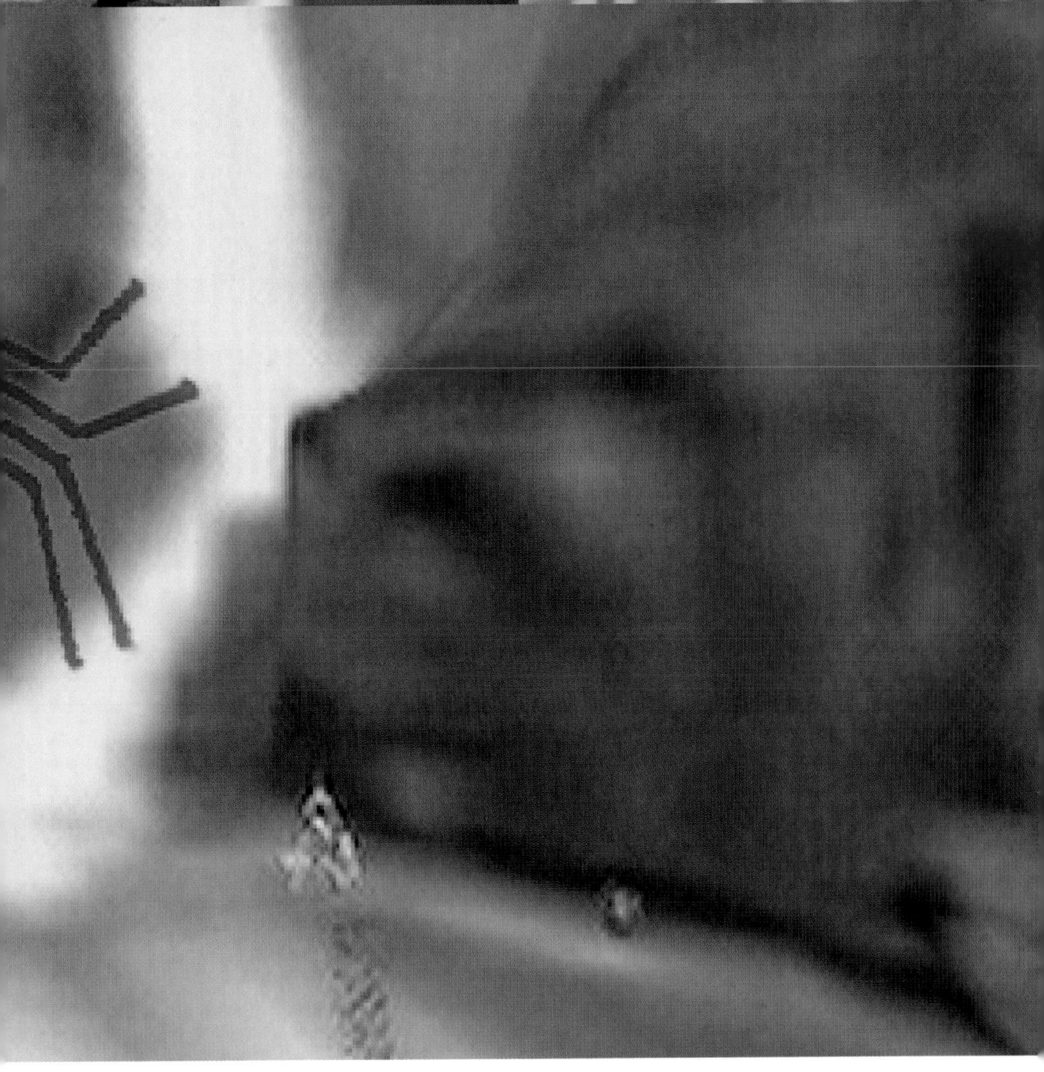

Placeholder

Time and motion are the underpinnings of animation and video. Though we're familiar with time and movement, we are usually unfamiliar with the design details used to craft an experience using animation and video. As with all other computer-enabled disciplines, novices quickly begin to appreciate that creating a satisfying design requires a wealth of time, experience, and knowledge—more than just access to a low-cost, powerful system for developing animation or editing video.

As with immersion, creating satisfying animation or video has as much to do with the cognitive or narrative solution as it does with the actual imagery. Experienced animators, for example, understand that the illusion of motion must be carefully created not just in slight changes from scene to scene but with characters and objects specifically drawn to imply motion and action. Likewise, cinematographers know that planned editing from scene to scene and view to view is almost as critical as the action caught by the camera.

Time and Motion

What differentiates successful video and animation is the care and appropriateness in illustrating motion and using the edits as a player in the story, which is just as important as lighting, acting, and costumes.

Another factor of time is in pacing; and this, like motion, is an element as critical as the subject matter itself. Alfred Hitchcock, for example, used timing and pacing in a film to create suspense in ways previously not conceived. Music videos use time and motion to create moods and influence emotions.

There is a visual literacy to timing, editing, and motion that we learn through experience. By the time we're young adults, we often take for granted the visual cues employed to tell a story—often used to tell it more efficiently. Just as we take for granted the act of talking to another person through a plastic, impersonal device like the telephone (something that babies must learn); so, too, do we take for granted the visual devices we've become accustomed to in the telling of stories on screen, such as close-ups, jump-cuts, establishing shots, and speed lines.

Time and Motion

Theater directors are always looking for innovative ways of involving their audiences, and new ways of creating an experience. Most have never thought to use or move through the space above their audience. At De La Guarda, there is no stage, only the space hanging above the audience, the walls, and the same floor where the audience stands. The performance begins with the audience standing shoulder-to-shoulder in a small room with a low ceiling. As the performance starts, the silhouettes of the performers move across the ceiling as the audience realizes that it is translucent. The ceiling then becomes a canvas of light, paint, objects, and people until it is finally punctured by the performers and, ultimately, destroyed—revealing a large, cavernous space above the audience.

This space is then a new kind of canvas that the performers hang, spin, and dance within (as well as on the walls) while creating narratives with movement and light. The performance is so captivating that the audience barely notices—if at all—crew and other performers moving into the crowd to begin new phases of the show. Soon, and for the duration of the production, the audience is dancing furiously along with the performers, interacting with them on the floor—and in the air.

de la Guarda

www.delaguarda.com

experience design 1.1

293

Interactive animation—especially when reactive to people moving and dancing—is a common theme but rarely well implemented. *Dancing in the Streets,* a project initiated by a York technology developer and a group at the University of Leeds, however, not only demonstrates how to blend live people and interactive systems but also how to create a satisfying experience that transforms otherwise disinterested or reluctant pedestrians into playful, expressive performers.

The system used a combination of motion detectors and projection equipment to track performers' movements in a defined area. The projections of animated graphics could then be aimed at these performers and respond to their movements within the space. In effect, this system was a co-creative dance environment allowing dancers to respond to and affect the animated projections.

These sorts of projected installations are now fairly commonplace in shopping malls and other public venues. However, rarely do these attractions offer this level of immersion or transformation. *Dancing in the Streets* controls lighting and animation to create a different kind of space that fills an area, instead of a simple "screen" projected on the

Dancing in the Streets   www.leeds.ac.uk/paci/projectingperformance/dancinginthestreets.html

floor. This care in crafting the installation is what transforms it into an experience that helps performers and participants forget their surroundings and contexts and "get lost" in the installation.

Part of the success of the project is due to the process in which it was created. By engaging professional dancers and performers, and by using performance and movement as part of the development process, the creators of this installation were able to experience the system while prototyping and make immediate changes based on how their bodies responded, rather than waiting for a traditional user testing phase later in the project. This performative process proved critical in adding and changing features to make the experience more interesting, clear, and intuitive for novice participants as it uncovered user needs and reactions during the early stages of development (which had to be completed in 6 weeks).

developers: Kit Monkman and Todd Wexler, KMA Creative Technologies, Ltd. Scott Palmer and Sita Popat, School of Performance & Cultural Industries, University of Leeds, 2005

Dancing in the Streets

Symbols can be used as a way of collapsing information into a smaller form. They also can be used as a mnemonic for the original information and can demonstrate or illustrate a process or identify something specific. What makes symbols powerful is their ability to transmit meaning under difficult circumstances—especially across linguistic and language barriers. However, just because something is a symbol, doesn't mean it automatically possesses the ability to communicate to everyone. Cultural differences make symbol, icon, and logo design even more risky and dangerous since they rely on much more shared context than other forms of communication. Not understanding the full range of meaning within a culture often causes designers to design symbols that not only fail to communicate what is intended, but often communicate false or defamatory information.

Symbolism

Where symbolism excels is when it is paired with other forms of communication (like a diagram or text label). This allows symbols to be more easily recognized and remembered (and used as a true mnemonic device). This is especially important for complex or critical information. Expecting a symbol or icon to function clearly on its own when representing new information or communicating to novices is probably asking too much of it.

Abstraction is also a difficult concept to communicate because abstract concepts, inherently, are more open to judgment, experience, and interpretation. Conceptual information relies heavily on personal contexts. However, when done well, this is precisely why abstraction can be so powerful; it can pull into an experience otherwise difficult or unconnected meanings that create a richer, more complex experience. This is also what great art does. These wider connections can lead to more emotional, personal, and surprising experiences that leave us more satisfied than representational experiences that simply "stick to the facts."

Symbolism

Disney's *The Lion King* is one of the most elaborate and beautiful spectacles of theater ever created. The musical production uses many untraditional theatrical techniques to tell the story of the lion cub, Simba. Director Julie Taymor uses the techniques of the Thai shadow puppets, Bunraku puppetry, and stark symbolism, which are more reminiscent of experimental theater, to create moods and convey an animal's characteristics, as well as to advance the story.

One of the first decisions Taymor made was not to conceal the actors in animal costumes. In fact, in most cases, the actors who portray animal characters (and those who act more as puppeteers) are revealed, making the costume design all the more radical and wonderful. When the full cast assembles on the stage at both the beginning and end of the production, the magnificence of the costumes and the way the actors and puppets move is astounding.

The Lion King

New Amsterdam Theater, New York City, NY
Pantages Theater, Los Angeles, CA
Lyceum Theater, London, England

Elsewhere in the musical, shadow puppets are used to connect the scenes in a natural bridge while the stage is reset (behind curtains) for the next scene. Not only is this form of storytelling economical, it also serves to add variety and a change in perspective for an audience that is more familiar with the changes of perspective and scale in television and movies than in theater (where, for example, close-ups are impossible).

Perhaps the most effective and symbolic storytelling comes at the moment in the story when the passing of time brings a severe drought. Rather than a voice-over explaining the amount of time passing and how bad the draught has become (a too commonly used technique), the curtains open on a large light blue circle of cloth covering the stage that is slowly pulled through a hole in the center of the stage. The metaphor is clear and powerful—and beautiful—without being overstated or obvious.

director and chief designer: Julie Taymor
date opened: 1993 (NYC)
www.disney.co.uk/MusicalTheatre/TheLionKing/
photographs: Joan Marcus

The Lion King

Early in the Web's history, Bank of America developed one of the first and biggest online banking sites. One of the challenges was to represent so many facets of such a large, complex organization that served many different constituents. The bank wanted to help each type of customer quickly get to the information and services they sought while still communicating to all that Bank of America was the sum of all of these distinct divisions.

Ketchum Communications, together with **vivid** studios, developed a website whose interface used the symbolism of blocks to communicate the message that Bank of America was the sum of many parts. This visual symbol was so powerful that it was used for three years, evolving somewhat in sophistication and message.

---

bankofamerica.com (1995-1998)

Ketchum team: Tim Bruns, Antonio Navas, Lawrence Stout, Susi Watson
vivid team: Steve deBrun, AnnD Canavan, Zeb Rice, Nathan Shedroff, Maurice Tani
Bank of America team: Karen Shapiro

BANK ONLINE!

HomeBanking
BankAmericard®

FREE online access to your bank, Visa® and MasterCard® accounts 24 hours a day! Now with a more convenient, unified password.

Learn More ——— Sign In

New and Notable:

- Buying a Home Today? Click here to save $200

* Win One of Three VW® New Beetles® in the VERSATEL® Check Card Triple Win Sweepstakes!

- Nominate an outstanding small business for an Enterprise Award. Entry deadline is July 10, 1998.

——— More News ———

the big day

Did you get married today? Jane and Robert MacMannes did. And they needed more than a wedding planner, they needed a financial planner.

people in motion

They found help, so can you. We can help from the first big day through the next 50 years, while you take care of other stuff.

Click on "Personal" for loans, credit cards, HomeBanking and much more.

Money Tip of the Day:

To help you put your money in motion.

——— See It ———

Interface Design...

Books

The Art of Human-Computer Interface Design, Brenda Laurel, editor, Addison-Wesley, 1990, ISBN 0201517973.

Apple Human Interface Guidelines: The Apple Desktop Interface, Apple Computer, Inc., Addison-Wesley, 1988, ISBN 0201177536.

The Design of Everyday Things, D.A. Norman, Basic Books, 1988, ISBN 0465067093.

A Natural History of the Senses, Diane Ackerman, Vintage Books, 1991, ISBN 0679735666.

The Meaning of Things: Domestic Symbols and the Self, Mihaly Csikszentmihalyi and Eugene Rochberg-Halton, Cambridge University Press, 1981, ISBN 052128774X.

Bringing Design to Software, Terry Winograd, editor, et al., Addison-Wesley, 1996, ISBN 0201854910.

Interface Culture, Steven A. Johnson, Harper San Francisco, 1997, ISBN 0465036805.

Organizations

ACM Multimedia, www.acm.org/sigmm

SHORE: University of Maryland Student HCI Online Research Experiments, www.otal.umd.edu/SHORE

SIGCHI (the Special Interest Group in Computer Human Interface issues of the Association of Computing Machinery) www.acm.org/sigchi

SIGGRAPH (the Special Interest Group in Computer Graphics of the Association of Computing Machinery), www.acm.org/siggraph

Conferences

CHI, www.acm.org/sigchi
SIGGRAPH, www.acm.org/siggraph

News

*ACM **interactions** Magazine,* www.acm.org/interactions
The SIGCHI Bulletin, www.acm.org/sigchi/bulletin

Other Resources

ACM Online Digital Library www.acm.org/dl
HCI Index is.twi.tudelft.nl/hci
HCI Resources usableweb.com

Information Design...

Books

Information Design, Robert Jacobson, Ph.D., Editor, MIT Press, 1999, ISBN 026210069X.

Information Architects, Richard Saul Wurman, Watson-Guptill Publishers, 1997, ISBN1888001380,

Information Anxiety, Richard Saul Wurman, Doubleday, 1989, ISBN 0553348566.

Information Anxiety 2, Richard Saul Wurman, Que, 2000, ISBN 0789724103.

Envisioning Information, Edward Tufte, Graphics Press, 1990, ISBN 0961392118.

The Visual Display of Quantitative Information, Edward Tufte, Graphics Press, 1983, ISBN 096139210X.

Hats, Richard Saul Wurman, *Design Quarterly* No.145, MIT Press, 1989.

The Age of Missing Information, Bill McKibben, Plume/Penguin, 1992, ISBN 0452269806.

Conferences

TED Conferences www.ted.com

Vision Plus Conferences www.vision-plus.net

Organizations

AIGA Experience Design, experiencedesign.aiga.org

International Institute for Information Design (IIID), Vienna, Austria (contact Peter Simlinger) www.iiid.net

Information Design PIC of the Society for Technical Communication stc.org/pics/idsig

Information Design Network www.csad.coventry.ac.uk/IDN

Resources
www.informationdesign.org

Information Design Resources www.xs4all.nl/~plato/InfoDesign.html

Information Architecture Resources www.jjg.net/ia

Rochester Institute of Technology Information Design Archive, design.rit.edu/DAO/main.html

Interaction Design...

Books

New Games, Andrew Fluegelman, Editor, Headlands Press Book, Dolphin/Doubleday, ISBN 038512516X.

Generation X, Douglas Coupland, St. Martin's Press (discussion of "Takeaways" on pages 91–104), 1992, ISBN 031205436X.

Life on the Screen: Identity in the Age of the Internet, Sherry Turkle, Simon & Shuster, 1997, ISBN 0684803534.

The Media Equation: How People Treat Computers, Television, and New Media Like Real People and Places, Byron Reeves and Clifford Nass, Cambridge University Press, 1998, ISBN 1575860538.

Tell Me a Story: Narrative and Intelligence, Roger C. Schank, Northwestern University Press, 1995, ISBN 0810113139

Influence: The Psychology of Persuasion, Robert B. Cialdini, Ph.D., Quill/William Morris, 1984, ISBN 0688128165.

Computers as Theater, Brenda Laurel, editor, Addison-Wesley, 1991, ISBN 0810113139.

Interactive Acting, Jeff Wirth, 1994, ISBN 0963237497.

Hosting Web Communities: Building Relationships, Increasing Customer Loyalty, and Maintaining A Competitive Edge, Cliff Figallo, John Wiley & Sons, 1998, ISBN 0471282936.

The Great Good Place: Cafes, Coffee Shops, Community Centers, Beauty Palors, General Stores, Bars, Hangouts and How They Get You Through the Day, Ray Oldenburg, Marlow & Co., 1989, ISBN 1569246815.

Resources

www.nathan.com/resources

Communities in Cyberspace, Marc Smith and Peter Kollock, Routledge, Editors, 1998, ISBN 0415191408.

The Virtual Community, Howard Rheingold, 2000 MIT Press, ISBN 0262681218

Smart Mobs, Howard Rheingold, 2002 Perseus Publishing, ISBN 0738206083 http://www.smartmobs.com

Design for Community, Derek Powazek, 2001 New Riders, ISBN 0735710759

Tell Me a Story: Narrative and Intelligence, Roger C. Schank, Northwestern University Press, 1995, ISBN 0810113139

Pause and Effect, Mark Meadows, 2002 New Riders, ISBN 0735711712

The Emperor of Scent, Chandler Burr, 2003 Random House, ISBN 0375759816

Making Meaning, Steve Diller, Nathan Shedroff, and Darrel Rhea, 2006 New Riders, ISBN 032137409

Online Articles

The Center for Digital Storytelling, www.storycenter.org

Online Community Articles
Online Community Report, www.onlinecommunityreport.com

Return on Community: Proving the Value of Online Communities in Business,www.participate.com/research/wp-return_on_community.asp

Building Profitable Community on the Web One Page at a Time, www.msnbc.com/news/151714.asp

There Goes the Neighborhood, Janelle Brown, www.salonmagazine.com/21st/feature/1999/01/cov_19feature.html

The Community is the Brand, Margaret Wertheim, www.laweekly.com/ink/00/28/cyber-wertheim.shtml

Conferences
DUX Conference, experiencedesign.aiga.org

Doors of Perception, www.mediamatic.com/doors

SIGCHI (the Special Interest Group in Computer Human Interface issues of the Association of Computing Machinery) www.acm.org/sigchi

SIGGRAPH (the Special Interest Group in Computer Graphics of the Association of Computing Machinery), www.acm.org/siggraph

Organizations
AIGA Experience Design, experiencedesign.aiga.org

Stanford University Project and People, Computers and Design, www-pcd.stanford.edu/pcd

Stanford CAPTology Lab, www.captology.org

MIT Media Lab, www.media.mit.edu

Institute for the Learning Sciences, www.ils.nwu.edu

The Center for Digital Storytelling, www.storycenter.org

The Improv Comedy Page, www.improvcomedy.org

ComedySportz Improv Comedy, www.teleport.com/~comedy

Good Experience, www.goodexperience.com

Hyper Island School of New Media, www.hyperisland.se

Visual Design...

Books
A Primer of Visual Literacy, Donis A. Dondis, MIT Press, 1973, ISBN 0262540290.

Design Yourself, Kurt Hanks, Larry Belliston, and Dave Edwards, Willam Kaufmann, Inc., 1978, ISBN 0913232386.

Experiences in Visual Thinking, Robert H. McKim, PWS Engineering, 1980, ISBN 0818504110.

Understanding Comics, Scott McCloud, Kitchen Sink Press, 1993, ISBN 0878162453.

Symbols Sourcebook, Henry Dreyfuss, McGraw-Hill, 1972, ISBN 0471288721.

The Icon Book: Visual Symbols for Computer Systems and Documentation, W. Horton, Wiley & Sons, 1994, ISBN 047159900X.

Handbook of Pictorial Symbols, Rudolf Modley, Dover Publications, Inc., 1977, ISBN 048623357X.

Signs + Emblems, Erhardt D. Stiebner and Dieter Urban, Van Nosrand Reinhold Company, ISBN 0442280599.

Dimensional Typography, J. Abbott Miller, Princeton Architectural Press, 1996, ISBN 1568980892.

The Photographer's Handbook, Third Edition, John Hedgecoe, Dorling/Kindersley, Knopf, 1992, ISBN 0679742042.

The Book of Video Photography, David Cheshire, Dorling/Kindersley, Knopf, ISBN 0394587448.

No Logo, by Naomi Klein, Picador, 2000, ISBN 0312271921.

Brand.New, Jane Pavitt, Editor, Princeton University Press, 2000, ISBN 069107061X

Selling the Invisible, Harry Beckwith, Warner Books, 1997, ISBN 0446520942.

Hey, Whipple, Squeeze This, Luke Sullivan, John Wiley & Sons, 1998, ISBN 0471293393.

Relationship Marketing, Regis McKenna, Addison-Wesley Publishing Company, Inc., 1993, ISBN 0201567695.

The 22 Immutable Laws of Marketing, Al Ries & Jack Trout, HarperBusiness, 1994, ISBN 0887306667.

Organizations
American Institute of Graphic Artists, www.aiga.org

Design Management Institute, www.designmgt.org

Online Resources
Visual Literacy Site, www.pomona.edu/visual-lit/intro/intro.html

Art and Culture, www.artandculture.com

Design Online, www.designonline.com

Resources

Index

Index

Index

Index

experience design 1.1

I can't thank enough the people who helped me put this book together...

my original editor, **Karen Whitehouse** who is the best editor I've ever met and with whom we share a mutual admiration society...

Michael Nolan who badgered me to consider writing this book in the first place...

my good friend **Laurie Blavin** who inispired my page designs and lent her photographts to the book...

Jeanne Stack and **Deniz Daldal** for putting-up with the production...

my friends and editorial board... **Steve deBrun, Abbe Don, BJ Fogg, Maria Giudice, Susanne Goldstein, Brenda Laurel, Davis Masten, Mark Meadows, Doris Mitch, Michael Everitt, Raoul Rickenberg, Jeff Wishnie**

my mother, **Phyllis Shedroff** and good friends **Norma Laskin** and **Gail Solomon** who were sure they wouldn't get mentioned in the book....

all photographs copyright Nathan Shedroff unless otherwise noted (not including screenshots, of course)...